Computer-Based Data Acquisition Systems

Design Techniques

James L. Taylor

Instrument Society of America

Computer-Based Data Acquisition Systems
DESIGN TECHNIQUES

Instrument Society of America
67 Alexander Drive, P.O. Box 12277
Research Triangle Park, NC 27709

Library of Congress Cataloging-in-Publication Data

Taylor, James L.
  Design techniques for scientific computer applications,
Data acquisition systems.

Bibliography: p.
  1. Process control — Data processing
  2. System design. I. Title.
TS156.8.T39   1986   660.2'81   85-23660
ISBN 0-87664-921-5

Design by Summit Technical Associates, Inc.

Dedicated to Yvonne

Preface

Several years ago as I was preparing for a design review meeting, I found that I had considerable difficulty in explaining to myself why certain components of a computer-based system had been chosen. The answers I gave myself as to why I had chosen a 12-bit ADC or why I had chosen Manufacturer A's transducers over Manufacturer B's were not technically defendable. Fortunately, no one at that review meeting asked me those questions. However, it was this incident that caused me to begin searching for a method whereby I could justify to myself and to others why a design had a particular form and why certain equipment had been chosen.

Today, answering these questions I had posed seems straightforward. There is a systematic way of designing a measurement system. There are methods that can help guide the engineer in his quest for answering the fundamental questions of "How accurate and how fast." The methods described in this book are intended to help answer only those two questions. The methods are not new — merely an engineering application of some fundamental concepts.

Over the years this material has been presented in various forms to numerous people at both seminars and short courses as well as to answer questions posed by younger engineers. The techniques advocated have always been well received. The enthusiastic response seemed to always revitalize my desire to complete this manuscript.

I am indebted to many people for their encouragement and help over the years. I was fortunate to have two mentors early in my career — Jim Lancaster and Marvin McKee. I am especially thankful to both for their patience and their guidance. More recently, Marvin's reviews and comments of the manuscript have been extremely beneficial in helping me to finalize this work. I am thankful to Sverdrup Technology, Inc., for presenting me the technical opportunities which led to this manuscript and to Sverdrup's management, especially Al Baer, Jim Uselton, Sam Pate and Jack Whitfield, for providing a professional environment that encourages and supports technical efforts such as this.

Over the years the manuscript has been revised and rewritten several times. I am grateful to Denise Whiteford and Barbara Pennington for their earlier typing and to Mary Young and Bill Crouch for the careful preparation of the graphics. Very special thanks go to Wanda Floyd. Wanda's efforts in typing, editing, drafting, encouraging, and doing whatever was needed to complete this manuscript have been superb.

Finally, thanks are due to my best friend and devoted wife Yvonne and to our two sons, David and Jimmy, for their patience and understanding. It would have been impossible to have completed this without their help.

Table of Contents

Chapter 1
Introduction to System Design

1.1 INTRODUCTION

The need to increase efficiency and improve quality, whether it be for a research and development facility that conducts experimental testing or for a manufacturing plant concerned with production levels and costs, has led to a proliferation of computer-based systems. Today, computer-based systems range from simple stand-alone personal computers or microprocessor-based systems to complete networks of minicomputers with large mainframe hosts. Such systems are used for numerous real-time applications including process control, process monitoring, and data acquisition. Partly because of the limited range of equipment manufactured by computer equipment vendors and partly because of unique requirements, many of the systems in use today represent a customized integration of equipment from different manufacturers. Accordingly, one of our primary concerns from a design viewpoint is with the process that is used in selecting this equipment. How does the designer go about choosing which sensors to use, what type of computer front-end equipment is needed, what sampling rates and interfaces are needed, and what are the required computer characteristics? How can you be assured that when the equipment is integrated to form the system its overall performance characteristics will satisfy the requirements? These are the fundamental questions that must be answered.

Our objectives with this manuscript are twofold. First, we want to develop a design approach that promotes a systematic design methodology. By this, we mean an approach that clearly describes how general requirements can be decomposed into specific hardware/software elements. Our second objective is to present analytical techniques that can be used to guide the systems engineer in establishing both a functional design and equipment specifications.

1.2 ESSENTIALS OF A DESIGN APPROACH

Design is an obscure process. It is obscure in that oftentimes we are asked to provide a system that will satisfy vaguely stated requirements (**Vague Requirements**). It is obscure in that oftentimes we "produce a design" yet have no recourse other than building and testing to ensure that the design will satisfy the requirements (**Questionable Approach**). It is ambiguous in that there are various terms (e.g., conceptual, functional, preliminary, final, detail) used to distinguish different phases of an unclear process. Unfortunately, these terms have different connotations that lead to misunderstandings as to what is to be done (**Vague Scope of Work**).

If we are to achieve the two objectives outlined previously, it is essential that first of all we formulate an approach that clarifies the system design process; and secondly, we identify or develop analytical techniques that can be used to bridge the gap between requirements and specifications. For our purposes, we consider system design to consist of two distinct phases — functional design and final design. As used here, functional design encompasses all activities necessary to establish requirements and to develop a system concept with well-defined performance characteristics that are traceable to the general requirements. Final design involves establishing all details necessary to implement functional design. With this distinction, we limit our attention to the functional design activity.

The first step in the functional design process is to establish requirements in concert with the user. While this appears intuitive, a great deal of care must be taken to insure that the requirements are comprehensive and do not impose severe constraints on the designer. It is our opinion that requirements involve much more than the technical aspects of the problem. For example, the end user's wants and desires must be considered, as well as all constraints. Thus, although there are numerous systems that will satisfy the criteria, some will be considered more acceptable than others. We want to stress at the beginning that regardless of how clever and ingenious a design may appear, it will in all probability meet resistance if the user thinks of the system as the designer's and not his. Consequently, the user must play an integral part in developing the requirements.

We can obtain some insight as to the next logical step by examining the form of our solution. For designers, the solution is a system. When we describe a system, we do so in terms such as accuracy, response, types of inputs and outputs, and cost. **The second step of the functional design process then is to translate the general requirements into specific system criteria.** We term this activity **analysis**. As we will see in later chapters, we concentrate on the fundamental criteria of accuracy, bandwidth, and performance as the basis of our analyses.

The third step in functional design involves establishing a functional configuration and equipment specifications. We use the results from the analyses as well as the non-technical requirements to establish the configuration and finalize specifications. It is at this stage in the design where we must address the remaining technical issues as well as the various social/economical and environmental issues. The result of this activity is a set of functional diagrams that establishes the form of our system and specifications that quantify major equipment performance.

1.3 A SYSTEMATIC APPROACH

The three steps listed previously constitute what we believe to be a systematic design approach. The approach enables the designer to develop a system by beginning with general requirements, using these to develop increasing levels of detail, and finally, establishing a configuration and selecting equipment. As a result of this methodology, the designer can adequately describe the rationale of both the system configuration and equipment selection process based on the user's general requirements.

As shown in Figure 1.1, the first step in the functional design process is to establish requirements that are consistent and complete, and not overly restrictive. For system design, this doesn't appear to be overly complex. We can get an idea of what criteria are needed for data systems by examining how such systems are characterized. Generally, this involves defining inputs, establishing accuracy and bandwidth requirements, analyzing the environment the system must operate in, and investigating other issues such as calibration, maintenance, and flexibility. While this may appear to be clear, it must be emphasized that establishing requirements is the fuzzy part of design. Certainly, we can determine whether the requirements are consistent and whether or not they are overly restrictive. We can not, however, easily ascertain their completeness.

It is at the completion of this initial step in the design process where the first formal review occurs between the user and the system engineer. The requirements are jointly reviewed and an understanding reached as to which of these are deemed critical and which are flexible. The requirements are critical since they form the basis for all subsequent design activities. Accordingly, we recommend that they be formalized. Once approved, the Requirements Document is used for quality control purposes. That is, the design is periodically checked and compliance demonstrated. In all likelihood, some requirements will change during functional design. Thus, a mechanism must be incorporated that enables changes to occur but only in a controlled and visible manner.

The second step of functional design is to analyze the general technical requirements to establish specific system criteria. To do this, we concentrate on accuracy, bandwidth, and global performance requirements. We apply error propagation techniques and systematic error budgeting to establish for each measurement the sensor accuracy and the accuracy characteristics for all analog system components such as signal conditioners, amplifiers, and filters. On an individual measurement basis, we quantify filter characteristics and sampling rates jointly to satisfy a sampling distortion and bandwidth requirement. We further quantify system criteria by analyzing the timing implications of global performance requirements.

The third step of functional design is to collectively consider the results of the individual measurement and timing analyses to establish the configuration. It is at this point in the functional design process where the solution takes form. Thus, we determine both the number and type of frontends and processors, specify their performance characteristics, and establish a functional software design specification.

Once the functional design has been completed and critically reviewed with respect to the requirements, the design is considered fixed and detail design can

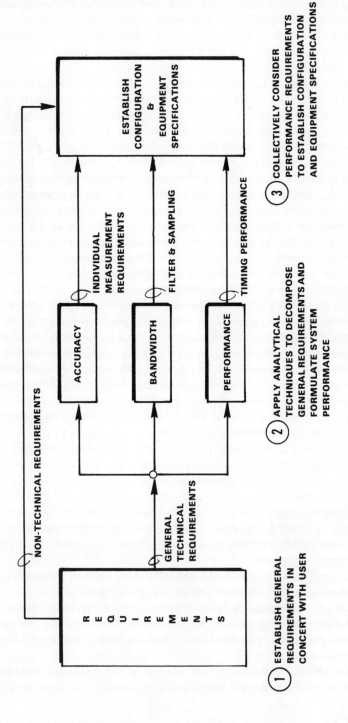

Figure 1.1. Functional Design Involves Three Distinct Steps

begin. By fixed, we mean that no further changes can be made without formal management approval. It is at the completion of this third step that the second formal design review occurs between the user and the system engineer. The purpose of this review, which is frequently termed the Preliminary Design Review, is to verify that the functional design does satisfy the Requirements. At this point, the system engineer must be able to rigorously defend the functional design and to demonstrate compliance with the Requirements.

1.4 SUMMARY

In this chapter, we established the need for a systematic design approach that would enable both the system configuration and equipment specifications to be established based on an analysis of the requirements. For computer-based systems used in real-time applications, the approach is critical for success. Waiting until a system is designed using conventional methods and then built to determine whether its integrated performance satisfies requirements is risky and in all likelihood will result in costly redesign or compromising of the requirements. Thus, we believe that the design approach should embrace analytical techniques that aid the designer in systematically decomposing requirements to establish equipment specifications.

In the following chapters, we develop analytical techniques based on two fundamental criteria — accuracy and bandwidth. Chapter 2 introduces fixed and random measurement error and establishes the concept of measurement uncertainty to account for the probabilistic nature of error. Chapter 3 concentrates on using error as a design criterion. Since systems are designed to produce information and since that information is based on one or more measurements, it is more logical to specify the required accuracy of the information rather than the individual measurement accuracies. Error propagation techniques are then used to establish individual measurement accuracy requirements. This same error technique is used to budget errors for the various system components. Chapter 4 presents an overview of the fundamentals of sampled data systems including signal conditioning and conversion and describes the various multiplexing methods used for multichannel systems. Chapter 5 presents the concepts of error models for several types of measurements and categorizes the different errors as fixed or random. Chapter 6 reviews the concepts of sampling and presents techniques that can be used to jointly establish anti-alias filter rolloff and sampling rate characteristics.

Chapter 7 describes the functional design process by considering composite measurement accuracy and sampling to establish the configuration and equipment specifications. Redundancy in this chapter with earlier chapters is intentional to bring together and reinforce fundamental concepts. Finally, we present comprehensive examples in the appendices, which are intended to illustrate more completely the analysis techniques.

Chapter 2
The Concept of Measurement Error

2.1 INTRODUCTION

Every measurement is in error. By this, we mean that there is always a discrepancy when the output of a system is compared to the input. Unfortunately, various terms are used somewhat interchangeably to describe this difference. These include accuracy, fixed and random error, systematic error, precision, resolution, and bias. Accordingly, there are numerous connotations to these terms that have perpetuated the miscommunication of what measurement error is and is not.

If our concern is only with measuring stationary phenomena, then the dynamic characteristics of the measurement system may be ignored. Accordingly, we can quantify the error whenever the input function is constant as a real number. Since we are concerned with making measurements over a range, $a \leq F \leq b$, and since it is unlikely that the error over this range would be constant, it is necessary to establish the error at various points throughout the measurement range. To accomplish this, we would perform an experiment whereby we could quantify the error at various discrete points representative of those within our range of measurement interest. For n discrete points, this would produce n discrete measures of error.

There are several ways of using our set of n error measures to describe system error. For example, we could describe error as the set of computed individual errors corresponding to the measured values. This would enable us to establish the error for any stated measurement value. For simplicity, however, it is desirable to characterize error in a more general sense. Alternatively then, we could select a single value of error from this set (e.g., the largest absolute value) and use this to represent measurement error. Over the entire measurement range this appears overly conservative and not representative of the magnitude of errors we typically would expect. It is thus desirable to select a method of characterizing error that is not overly restrictive and less arbitrary. Accordingly, we look to statistics as a means of achieving this.

2.2 RANDOM ERROR

2.2.1 Characterizing Error Statistically

We can quantify system measurement error by applying known inputs and observing the response. Figure 2.1 illustrates the relationship between input and output.

Ideally, the output would exactly match the input producing no error. At each discrete input, error is defined as the difference between input and output. If our experiment consisted of *n* different inputs, we would have *n* different measures of error, which we postulate would have a probability distribution function as shown in Figure 2.2.

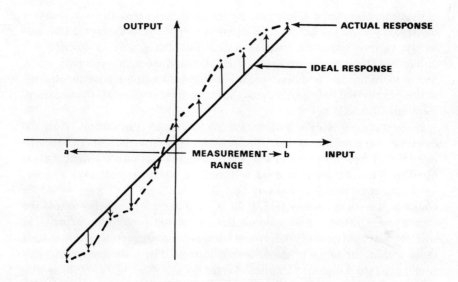

Figure 2.1. Measurement System Input/Output Relationship

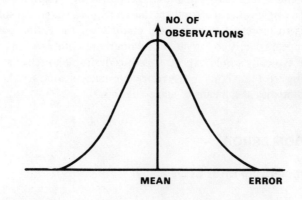

Figure 2.2 Error Distribution Function

Here the distribution is assumed Gausian or normal. As such, most errors are small and appear clustered about the mean. The statistical relationship between error magnitude and probability can be expressed in terms of a parameter called **standard deviation**.

Standard deviation is a statistic computed from the set of measurement errors that describes the scatter or variability of measurement error. If our set of n experimentally determined errors are denoted e_i for i equals 1 to n, then the standard deviation for this set of samples can be computed as:

$$S = \left[\frac{\sum\limits_{i=1}^{n} (e_i - \bar{e})^2}{n - 1} \right]^{1/2} \tag{2.1}$$

where $\bar{e}$ is the arithmetic mean computed as:

$$\bar{e} = \frac{\sum\limits_{i=1}^{n} e_i}{n} \tag{2.2}$$

If we assume our measurement errors have a normal distribution, we can statistically discuss measurement error probability. For example, Figure 2.3 illustrates a normal error distribution. If we are interested in determining what

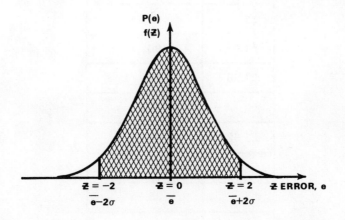

**Figure 2.3 Area Under Normal Probability Curve
is a Function of σ, Standard Deviation**

the probability is that the error will lie within this shaded area, it is necessary to determine the area under the normal probability curve between $Z = -2$ and $Z = 2$. This can be computed by evaluating the following integral:

$$f(Z) = \frac{1}{\sqrt{2\pi}} \int_{-2Z}^{2Z} e^{-Z^2/2} \, dZ \qquad (2.3)$$

where

$$Z = \frac{e - \bar{e}}{\sigma} \qquad (2.4)$$

and σ is the population standard deviation. Thus, the area under the curve is a function of σ, the population's standard deviation.

Since we are interested in discussing error in terms of probability, we can state that we are confident that a measurement error will lie within this shaded area. Our level of confidence is equal to the shaded area under the curve and is expressed in percent. Table 2.1 lists confidence level as a function of the parameter Z.

Table 2.1. Confidence Level as a Function of Z

Z	CONFIDENCE, %
±1.	68.26
±1.645	90.
±1.96	95.
±2.	95.46
±2.326	98.
±2.576	99.
±3.	99.74
±3.291	99.9
±3.891	99.99

As an example, we can state that our error, e_t, is:

$$e_t = \bar{e} \pm 2S \tag{2.5}$$

At this value, we are 95.46 percent confident that any measurement error, e_i, will be within the interval

$$\bar{e} - 2S \leq e_i \leq \bar{e} + 2S \tag{2.6}$$

Alternatively, we can state that there is approximately a 5 percent probability that a measurement error will lie outside this range. Any desired confidence value can be achieved by simply selecting the standard deviation multiplier that corresponds to the desired probability.

Assuming that the errors are normally distributed, the standard deviation statistic enables us to characterize a set of measurement errors. Ideally, our set of measurement errors would exhibit very little scatter, thus producing a relatively small value of S. The term commonly used to describe this scattering phenomena is precision. Thus, we say that measurement systems that exhibit small values of S are more precise than those that exhibit large values of S.

Example 2.1

Assume that we are performing an experiment to determine the static performance characteristics of an amplifier. As shown in the sketch below, we are applying known inputs to the amplifier with a precision voltage standard and observing its response with a precision voltmeter. For the purpose of this example, we assume that there are no errors associated with either the voltage source or the voltmeter.

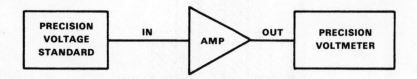

**Experimental Setup to Establish Static
Performance Characteristics of Amplifier**

The inputs and corresponding amplifier outputs (normalized for the gain setting) are presented below in tabular form.

INPUT	OUTPUT/GAIN	ERROR=INPUT-OUTPUT/GAIN
0	0.003	-0.003
1	1.006	-0.006
3	2.995	+0.005
5	4.990	+0.010
7	7.015	-0.015
9	9.020	-0.020
7	7.005	-0.005
5	4.995	+0.005
3	3.005	-0.005
1	1.008	-0.008
0	0.002	-0.002

A histogram of the errors is presented in the sketch below.

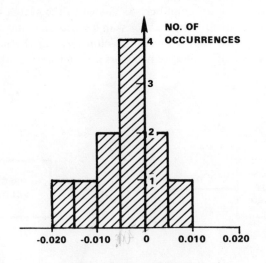

Amplifier Error Histogram

For this example, the mean error is computed using Equation 2.2 as −0.004 and the sample standard deviation using Equation 2.1 as 0.009. Using Equation 2.5 we can state that we are 95 percent confident that the measurement error at any point will be equal to or less than

$$e_t = -0.004 \pm 2(0.009)$$

Thus, the range of errors for a 95 percent confidence level is

$$-0.022 \leq e \leq 0.014$$

2.2.2 Relating Sample Statistics to the Population

In our examples thus far, we have not made a distinction between sample standard deviation, S, and population standard deviation, δ. It is of interest to note that if we were to construct an error distribution function from a sample set of errors, the distribution would appear as a histogram (Figure 2.4). As our sample size became larger, we would further subdivide the error brackets. As the sample size n approaches infinity, the sample error distribution would approach the normal error distribution.

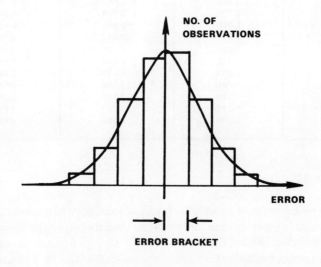

Figure 2.4. Sample Error Histogram

Our concern here is in deciding how well the standard deviation(s), computed using a finite sample of size n, approximates the population standard deviation σ. It is of interest to note that in 1907 W.S. Gosset, an English chemist who at that time was a student, had a similar concern. Gosset determined that the sample standard deviation underestimated the population standard deviation. Subsequently, he developed a table of multipliers that could be used to artificially inflate the sample standard deviation and thus reduce the risk associated with estimating σ using S. The table, which is based on both the sample size and the confidence level, is referred to in statistics texts as the Student T distribution.

In quantifying measurement error, we are always working with a sample extracted from the total population. Accordingly, we would compute the sample mean and standard deviation using Equations 2.1 and 2.2. However, rather than using the value of two as a multiplier for S as we did earlier, we would select the multiplier from the Student T table (see Table 2.2) based on both the sample size and desired degree of confidence.

Table 2.2. Condensed Student T Distribution

DEGREES OF FREEDOM df	CONFIDENCE LEVEL: $1 - \alpha$		
	0.900	0.950	0.990
1	6.314	12.706	63.657
2	2.920	4.303	9.925
3	2.353	3.182	5.841
4	2.132	2.776	4.604
5	2.015	2.571	4.032
6	1.943	2.447	3.707
7	1.895	2.365	3.499
10	1.812	2.228	3.169
15	1.753	2.131	2.947
20	1.725	2.086	2.845
30	1.697	2.042	2.750
60	1.671	2.000	2.660
∞	1.645	1.960	2.576

Example 2.2

In Example 2.1, we used a multiplier for S of 2 to achieve 95 percent confidence. However, since we are using a sample rather than the total population, we need to select a multiplier from the Student T table. Using a degree of freedom value of 10, the correct multiplier for 95 percent confidence is 2.228. Thus, the error is

$$e_t = -0.004 \pm 2.228(0.009)$$

The corresponding range is

$$-0.024 \leq e \leq 0.016$$

From this, we can see that the error range is slightly extended because we are using a limited sample size.

2.2.3 Other Variability Effects

In the previous subsections, we established that there was a variability of error over a measurement range. That is, if we were interested in characterizing measurement error over the range $a \leq m \leq b$, we would experimentally determine the error at n discrete points throughout this range. At each point, we would compute error as the difference between input and output. We assumed that this sample set of n errors came from a normal distribution. This enabled us to compute the sample standard deviation, relate the sample statistic to the population standard deviation using the Student T distribution and any desired confidence level, and thus establish a probable error interval.

It is of interest to inquire as to whether or not there would be any measurement error variability if we were only interested in making measurements at one specific point. The answer to that is yes. At any point, the repeatability of the measurement is influenced by the following:

- hysteresis
- electrical noise
- time variations of the measurement
- thermal drift
- cross talk
- common mode voltage

This potential list of random errors, which is not intended to be all inclusive, indicates the complexity associated with quantifying the random nature of errors. Fortunately, we can quantify the effects of several of these through carefully designed and conducted experiments. Since we expect that the error at any point will vary, the experiment must be designed to make multiple measurements at each point. Thus, if we are interested in establishing measurement error over the range $a \leq m \leq b$, we would select n points. At each point, we would make multiple readings and use these to establish error at that point. Errors at each point and throughout the range would then be pooled and used to compute sample standard deviation and thus precision.

2.3 FIXED ERROR

2.3.1 Bias

If at a measurement value we make repeated measurements and compare each of these to the true known value, we will observe some variability in the measurements as previously discussed. Additionally, it is probable that each measurement will be in error by a fixed amount. This fixed difference between the true value and the average of all repeated measurements is shown in Figure 2.5 and is referred to as bias.

Since we have been able to quantify bias, we can eliminate this fixed error through compensation. That is,

$$\text{BIAS} = \text{AVG VALUE} - \text{TRUE VALUE} \tag{2.7}$$

Thus, for this example where we have indicated bias as a positive value, we can reduce each measurement by the computed bias. This will have the effect of forcing the average measured value to equal the true value (Figure 2.6). We can then state that for this example we are 95 percent confident that any measurement we make within the range will lie in the interval

$$\text{True Value} - 2S \leq m \leq \text{True Value} + 2S \tag{2.8}$$

Alternatively, we can state that the error at this measurement value is $\pm 2S$.

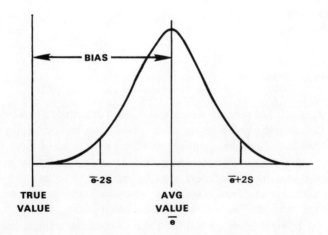

Figure 2.5. The Effect of Positive Fixed Errors in Each Measurement

Example 2.3

In Example 2.1, we computed an average error of –0.004 by assuming that no errors were introduced by either the voltage source or the voltmeter. For this example, the average error of –0.004 represents a fixed error. Since we have been able to quantify the bias, we can compensate each reading accordingly. Thus, we would algebraically subtract the bias of –0.004 from each element in the error column of Example 2.1. This effectively reduces the mean error to zero.

2.3.2 Classes of Bias

To compute bias, it is required that we know the true value. Unfortunately, the true value is sometimes elusive and thus not always quantifiable. This is a consequence of the fact that there are two classes of fixed errors that affect the true value — known and unknown biases.

Known biases are those that become quantifiable through calibration. Depending upon the magnitude and upon the complexities associated with compensating for this, we may elect not to apply any compensation. Thus, we knowingly tolerate a measurement bias.

As we stated, we must know the true value to establish bias. Generally speaking, we are using secondary or working standards rather than primary standards in our experiment. Accordingly, there is in all probability some fixed but unknown error associated with the calibration hierarchy, which we assume to be negligible.

A second and potentially more serious source of unknown bias errors are those attributable to human errors and environmental effects. Unfortunately, there is no way to eliminate these. However, with proper engineering and installation practices, we can reduce their probability.

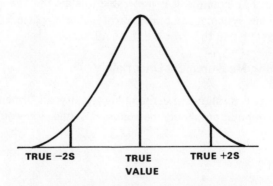

Figure 2.6. Measurements Centered About the True Value when Bias Eliminated

2.4 MEASUREMENT UNCERTAINTY

2.4.1 Computing Uncertainty

In the previous subsections, we have determined that there are two components of measurement error — precision and bias. As used here, precision is a statistic, whereas bias is at best an estimate of fixed error based on engineering judgment. While drastically different, both are components of measurement error and therefore must be combined in some acceptable manner if we are to quantify measurement error.

One technique for quantifying measurement error, which is gaining widespread acceptance, is to use the bias limit plus some multiple of precision to compute measurement uncertainty, U. In its simplest form, uncertainty to a confidence level of $1 - \alpha$ can be stated as:

$$U = \pm (B + t_\alpha S) \tag{2.9}$$

where t_α is the Student T multiplier.

Here, we have used a single number to estimate both positive and negative bias. However, it may be that we can establish different values (e.g., B_1 and B_2) for negative and positive bias limits. Thus, our measurement uncertainty would be stated as:

$$-(B_1 + t_\alpha S) \leq U \leq + (B_2 + t_\alpha S) \tag{2.10}$$

Another acceptable method (see Example 2.2) of stating uncertainty is:

$$B - t_\alpha S \leq U \leq B + t_\alpha S \tag{2.11}$$

In any case, measurement uncertainty reflects the probabilistic nature of measurement error. Accordingly, we should attach a confidence level to any number stated. For example, it is preferable to state that we are 95 percent confident that any system measurement error will be less than $\pm 0.1\%$ full scale rather than to state that the error is $\pm 0.1\%$ full scale.

2.4.2 Reporting Measurement Uncertainty

Because there is no standard defining uncertainty, all elements used in the uncertainty computation should be reported. Thus, we would report the following:

- Bias Limit(s) — B
- Precision — S
- Confidence Level — $1 - \alpha$
- Degrees of Freedom — df

As used here, degrees of freedom relate to the number of samples used in establishing S and is computed as:

$$df = \text{Number of Samples} - 1 \tag{2.12}$$

Reporting error in this form not only enables others to redefine measurement uncertainty as they determine best for their application, but it also enables the errors from one system to be combined with the errors from other systems.

2.5 COMBINING ERRORS

2.5.1 Establishing Total Bias and Precision Using the Root-Sum-Square Technique

The ideal way to determine measurement uncertainty is to perform a single experiment on the entire system. While this may be ideal, it generally is not practical. For example, we may have a system consisting of various types of sensors and a common data system. For such a system, we may elect to have all sensors calibrated in a laboratory and calibrate the data system in place. In accordance with our definition of measurement uncertainty, we would then have separate values of B, S, α, and df for the sensor and the data system. Thus, to establish total measurement uncertainty for any sensor channel, we need to combine the measurement errors of both the sensor and the data system.

There are various ways that the errors could be combined. For example, we could simply add the errors. However, this is overly conservative, especially when we consider that in all probability some cancellation of errors would occur. One widely accepted technique for combining errors that allows for some cancellation is the Root-Sum-Square (RSS) technique.

To apply the RSS, we simply take the square root of the sum of squares for each error component. That is, we would compute total bias and precision as follows:

$$B_T = \left[B_1^2 + B_2^2 \right]^{1/2} \tag{2.13}$$

$$S_T = \left[S_1^2 + S_2^2 \right]^{1/2} \tag{2.14}$$

where the subscript 1 is used to indicate sensor errors and the subscript 2 to indicate data system errors. As before, there are other techniques that can be used for computing total system bias such as selecting the largest absolute value. However, since there are no standards, it is left up to the discretion of the experimenter as to which technique to use. Here, we use the RSS for combining bias as well as precision.

2.5.2 Establishing Total Uncertainty

As before, uncertainty is computed as the bias limit plus a multiple of precision that corresponds to the desired confidence level. That is,

$$U_T = \pm (B_T + t_\alpha S_T) \qquad\qquad 2.15$$

where B_T and S_T are as defined by Equations 2.13 and 2.14. To establish t_α, we need to compute the equivalent degrees of freedom corresponding to df_1 and df_2 and use this with the Student T distribution.

There are various methods for establishing the equivalent degrees of freedom. Two such techniques are:

$$DF = \left(\sum_{i=1}^{n} df_i \right) - n \qquad\qquad (2.16)$$

$$DF = \frac{\left[\sum_{i=1}^{n} S_i^2 \right]^2}{\sum_{i=1}^{n} \dfrac{S_i^4}{df_i}} \qquad\qquad (2.17)$$

where for both techniques, n denotes the number of individual error sources. Once the equivalent degrees of freedom have been computed, this value, in conjunction with the desired confidence α, is used to determine the appropriate value of t_α.

Example 2.4

As an example of combining errors using the RSS technique, consider that we have performed an experiment on an analog-to-digital converter (ADC) and established the ADC's error characteristic in a manner similar to that used for our amplifier (Example 2.1). We would like to determine the error characteristics for the amplifier-ADC combination. The sketch below indicates the configuration and the experimentally determined bias and precision for each element.

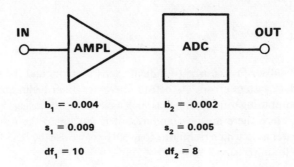

$b_1 = -0.004$	$b_2 = -0.002$
$s_1 = 0.009$	$s_2 = 0.005$
$df_1 = 10$	$df_2 = 8$

Applying the RSS technique, we compute system bias and precision as follows:

$$B = \left[b_1^2 + b_2^2 \right]^{1/2} = 0.0044$$

$$S = \left[S_1^2 + S_2^2 \right]^{1/2} = 0.0103$$

The equivalent degrees of freedom are computed using both techniques as:

1. $df = (df_1 + df_2) - 2 = 16$

2. $df = \dfrac{\left[S_1^2 + S_2^2 \right]^2}{\dfrac{S_1^4}{df_1} + \dfrac{S_2^4}{df_2}} = 15.3$

System uncertainty, U, is then computed as:

$$U = \pm(B + t_{95}S)$$

Using an equivalent degrees of freedom of 16, the value of t_{95} is 2.122. Thus,

$$U = \pm[0.0044 + (2.122)(0.0103)] = \pm 0.026$$

Accordingly we are 95% confident that the error introduced in the measurement will lie somewhere within the interval of ± 0.026.

2.6 SUMMARY

As we have seen in this chapter, measurement error consists of both fixed and random components and thus should be viewed as a probabilistic rather than a deterministic parameter. The term measurement uncertainty, which we have defined as a combination of bias and precision, is more descriptive of measurement errors since it has a connotation of probability. While this definition is gaining widespread acceptance, it is not a standard. Accordingly, engineers are free to define and report error as they determine best for their application. Regardless of the definition used, measurement error should not be viewed as an absolute since measurement error constituents and their magnitude are subject to variations. The difficulty of identifying all possible error sources and then quantifying them strengthens the argument for referring to measurement error as measurement uncertainty.

Oftentimes, users are interested in relative rather than absolute accuracy. This is especially true for those applications where the experimental testing is comparative. That is, an experiment is conducted, a change is made, the experiment repeated, and the results of the two experiments compared to determine if the change made was significant. For this type of testing, bias can be assumed to be the same for both experiments and thus can be ignored. A possible problem with this approach is that the large unknown biases, resulting from either environmental effects or human errors and which we assume to be zero, may in fact vary. While we may elect not to quantify bias, it is critical that we acknowledge the possible existence and take proper precaution to minimize the effects.

Chapter 3
Error as a Fundamental Design Criterion

3.1 PERFORMANCE PARAMETERS

Measurements are made for the purpose of producing information that can be used for decision making. While it is true that we often make measurements to monitor the operational status of equipment or a process, even these measurements are considered to produce information. Here, the information may simply be that the equipment/process is operating properly or not. In the event that the information indicates abnormal operation, we execute some course of action. In contrast to this monitoring class of information, we make measurements and use these to produce information that quantifies or documents the results of an experiment. The term used here to describe this second classification is **performance parameter**.

For either classification, we must be concerned about the accuracy of the measurements used to produce that information. Since there are uncertainties associated with each measurement, there must then be some uncertainty associated with the information that is produced using those measurements. Because decisions are made based on that information, it becomes essential that we quantify the effects of measurement uncertainties and thus establish an uncertainty interval for each performance parameter.

As an example, consider a performance parameter F, which is a function of the measurement m_1. At a point P^0, where $m_1 = m_1^0$, there is a measurement uncertainty for m_1 of Δm_1. As shown in Figure 3.1, F can then take on a wide range of values (δF^0) corresponding to the uncertainty for m_1. Figure 3.1 also illustrates the range of values ($\delta F'$) that F takes on at a second point (P') within the range. At this point, Δm_1 is the same, but the corresponding change in F is greater. Thus we see that the effects of the measurement uncertainty on the function F is variable and depends upon the sensitivity of F at the point in question.

To a first-order approximation, the change in F, denoted δF, can be established by multiplying the slope at the point in question by the total change in m_1 (Δm_1). That is,

$$\delta F \approx \frac{dF}{dm_1} \Delta m_1 \tag{3.1}$$

Graphically, we can represent this by constructing a tangent to the curve at the point in question and extending this such that it intersects the upper and lower boundary for Δm_1 at that point. The two corresponding parameter values at these intersections define the uncertainty in F, denoted as δF, which is attributable to the uncertainty in m_1.

If, instead of a function involving one measurement, we have a performance parameter that is a function of n measurements, we must be concerned with how errors in all n measurements will affect the parameter. To quantify these effects, we need to explore about a point and establish the sensitivity of the function to each measurement. The mathematical technique that allows this exploration to be accomplished is the Taylor series expansion. For example, consider the function

$$F = f(m_1, m_2 \ldots, m_n) \tag{3.2}$$

If at a point P, defined as $f(m_1^0, m_2^0, \ldots, m_n^0)$, the function and its partial derivatives are continuous, then the change in F (denoted as δF), which results from changes in the n measurements (Δm_i), can be stated as

$$\delta F = \left.\frac{\partial f}{\partial m_1}\right|^0 \Delta m_1 + \left.\frac{\partial f}{\partial m_2}\right|^0 \Delta m_2 + \ldots + \left.\frac{\partial f}{\partial m_n}\right|^0 \Delta m_n + R \tag{3.3}$$

where the partial derivatives, $\dfrac{\partial f}{\partial m_i}$, are to be evaluated at the point P, and the remainder term R contains all higher-order and cross-product partial derivatives. If F were a function of one measurement rather than n measurements, the above expression remains valid and the partial derivative becomes the total

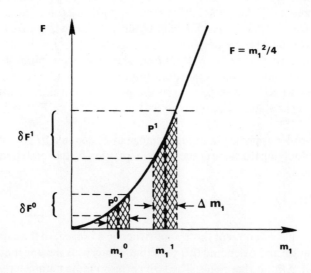

**Figure 3.1. Effects of Measurement Errors (m_1)
on Parameter F at Different Points**

derivative. That is,

$$\frac{\partial f}{\partial m_1} = \frac{df}{dm_1} \tag{3.4}$$

Accordingly,

$$\delta F = \frac{df}{dm_1} \Delta m_1 \tag{3.5}$$

which is what we established previously.

At this point, we need to reconsider the nature of the Δm_i terms. Here, the Δm_i are measurement errors and consist of a fixed number for bias and some multiple of the standard deviation for precision. Thus, each Δm_i has a distribution (we assume this to be the normal error distribution), which is centered about some average error. Typically, the numbers we would quote for each Δm_i would be the measurement uncertainty interval corresponding to some desired level of confidence. If we use these uncertainty limits as the Δm_i and if all the evaluated partials have the same sign, we are assuming the worst case. In all likelihood, there will at any time be some positive and negative measurement errors, and thus we would anticipate some cancellation of errors to occur. Accordingly, one technique that allows for some error cancellation is the root-sum-square technique. For this technique,

$$\delta F = \pm \left[\left(\frac{\partial f}{\partial m_1} \bigg|^0 \Delta m_1 \right)^2 + \left(\frac{\partial f}{\partial m_2} \bigg|^0 \Delta m_2 \right)^2 + \ldots + \left(\frac{\partial f}{\partial m_n} \bigg|^0 \Delta m_n \right)^2 \right]^{1/2}$$

$$\tag{3.6}$$

Here again, there is no standard method for combining errors, and thus the engineer may select some alternative method. If the consequences associated with making a wrong decision based on δF are significant, a more conservative method may be appropriate.

Example 3.1

Problem Statement

Brake Specific Fuel Consumption (BSFC) is a critical parameter used to quantify engine performance and is defined by the following equation:

$$\text{BSFC} = (CF)/(TN)$$

where F is fuel flow, T is engine torque, N is engine speed, and C is a constant. Determine allowable measurement errors for fuel flow, torque, and speed that will ensure that the uncertainty in BSFC is less than 1 percent at the point defined by

N = 2400 rpm
F = 4.32 lb/hr
T = 8.8 lb-ft
C = 5252

Solution

In general notation, the parameter BSFC can be stated as

$$\text{BSFC} = f(F, T, N)$$

Expanding in a Taylor series yields

$$\delta\text{BSFC} = \frac{\partial f}{\partial F}\, \Delta F + \frac{\partial f}{\partial T}\, \Delta T + \frac{\partial f}{\partial N}\, \Delta N + R$$

Assuming the remainder R is zero, then applying the RSS,

$$\delta\text{BSFC} = \left[\left(\frac{\partial f}{\partial F}\Delta F\right)^2 + \left(\frac{\partial f}{\partial T}\Delta T\right)^2 + \left(\frac{\partial f}{\partial N}\Delta N\right)^2\right]^{\frac{1}{2}}$$

where ΔF, ΔT, and ΔN, represent measurement errors and δBSFC is the uncertainty in BSFC resulting from the three measurement errors. The partial derivatives are:

$$\frac{\partial f}{\partial F} = \frac{C}{TN} = \frac{\text{BSFC}}{F}$$

$$\frac{\partial f}{\partial T} = \frac{-CF}{T^2N} = \frac{-\text{BSFC}}{T}$$

$$\frac{\partial f}{\partial N} = \frac{-CF}{TN^2} = \frac{-\text{BSFC}}{N}$$

At the point where $F = 4.32$, $T = 8.8$, $N = 2400$, the parameter BSFC is computed to be 1.074. Evaluating the above partials at this point yields

$$\frac{\partial f}{\partial F} = 0.2486$$

$$\frac{\partial f}{\partial T} = -0.122$$

$$\frac{\partial f}{\partial N} = -4.5 \times 10^{-4}$$

using calculus

Substituting these into the expression for BSFC yields

$$\delta \text{BSFC} = \left[(0.2486)^2 \, \Delta F^2 + (-0.122)^2 \, \Delta T^2 + (-4.5 \times 10^{-4})^2 \, \Delta N^2 \right]^{1/2}$$

To achieve 1 percent uncertainty in BSFC, we must allocate measurement errors ΔF, ΔT, and ΔN to satisfy the following relationship:

$$1.15 \times 10^{-4} = 0.062 \Delta F^2 + 0.015 \Delta T^2 + 2.0 \times 10^{-7} \Delta N^2$$

Here we have one equation in three unknowns. Thus, we can choose any two and have the third defined.

At this point we can determine the maximum error for each measurement by assuming that all uncertainty in the parameter BSFC is the result of error in one measurement. For example, we do this by assuming first that only fuel flow is in error and the torque and speed measurement errors are zero. We then repeat this for the other two combinations. Applying this technique, the maximum error limits for each measurement are computed to be:

$$\Delta F = 0.043$$
$$\Delta T = 0.088$$
$$\Delta N = 24$$

The δBSFC error relationship involves ΔN, ΔF, and ΔT. At the point where $F = 4.32$, $T = 8.8$, and $N = 2400$, the quadratic relationship can be graphically illustrated as a surface with the intersections as defined above. Obviously, there is an infinite number of points $(\Delta N^0, \Delta F^0, \Delta T^0)$ within this solid that, if chosen, will satisfy the 1 percent uncertainty in BSFC.

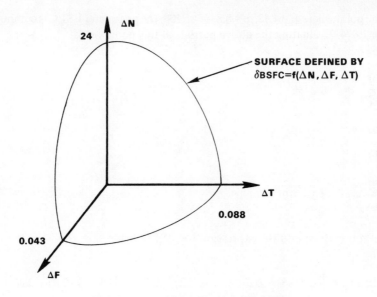

Measurement Error Surface for BSFC

For simplicity, we can restrict our attention to two variables. Assuming the error in speed is negligible, we have the following relationship:

$$1.15 \times 10^{-4} = 0.062\Delta F^2 + 0.015\Delta T^2$$

which is plotted below for positive ΔF and ΔT. For simplicity, the plot is restricted to the first quadrant.

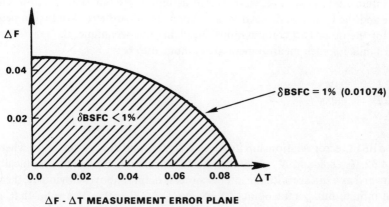

ΔF - ΔT MEASUREMENT ERROR PLANE
(ΔF = 0.043, ΔT = 0.088)

Here the intersections (ΔF = 0.043, ΔT = 0.088) are the points computed above, and the arc connecting the intersections is the quadratic expression for δBSFC.

Example 3.2

Problem Statement

In Example 3.1, we used calculus to establish algebraic expressions for the partial derivatives. There are, however, occasions when the complexity of the performance parameter suggests that numerical approximation of the partials is more convenient. Determine the partials numerically for Example 3.1 and compare the results to those obtained using calculus.

Solution

At the base set of conditions

N = 2400
F = 4.32
T = 8.8

BSFC was computed to be 1.074. We approximate $\partial f / \partial F$ by letting the flow measurement F have an incremental change δF

$$F' = F + \delta F$$

while maintaining N and T at the base values. We compute the new value of BSFC at F', N, and T. That is,

$$\text{BSFC}' = f(F', N, T)$$

We then compute our approximation for the partial derivative as:

$$\frac{\partial f}{\partial F} \approx \frac{\Delta \text{BSFC}}{\Delta F} = \frac{\text{BSFC}' - \text{BSFC}}{F' - F}$$

In the limit as δF approaches zero, our numerical approximation will approach the partial derivative. Thus, our first concern is with choosing a value for δF. Unfortunately, the only way to do this without prior knowledge of the partials is by trial and error. Thus, one would compute the partial for several different values of F and select a δF where the change in the numerically computed partial was insignificant.

3.2 ESTABLISHING INDIVIDUAL MEASUREMENT ERROR BASED ON PERFORMANCE PARAMETER SPECIFICATIONS

As we have stated, measurements are made to establish information. Thus, if our task is to design a measurement system, a natural beginning point for the design process is to examine the performance parameter relationships. That is, we need to determine which measurements are required and why. For each performance parameter, we would expand the function F_i in a Taylor series to establish the relationship between measurement error, Δm_j, and performance parameter criteria δF_i as described in Section 3.1. At a point P defined by $(m_1^0, m_2^0, \ldots, m_n^0)$ the partials can be evaluated producing

$$\delta F_i = a_1 \Delta m_1 + \ldots + a_n \Delta m_n \tag{3.7}$$

where

$$a_k = \left. \frac{\partial f_i}{\partial m_k} \right|^0 \tag{3.8}$$

indicates that each partial is to be evaluated at the point P. Since δF_i is specified at the point P, the above represents a linear equation in n unknowns. Application of the RSS technique yields:

$$\delta F_i^2 = a_1^2 \Delta m_1^2 + \ldots + a_n^2 \Delta m_n^2 \tag{3.9}$$

Thus, at the point P, we have established the desired relationship between measurement errors, Δm_n, and the performance parameter specification δF_i.

It should be emphasized that unless the partials are constants the above relationship is valid only at a single point. Accordingly, since we are generally concerned about performance parameters over a range $a \le F_i \le b$, we must select the point that produces the maximum error. That is, while the relationship may be valid over a wide range, our concern is only at one specific point within the range.

In the simplest form, the system we are to design consists of one performance parameter, which is a function of n measurements denoted m_n. Application of the above will produce a nonlinear relationship in n unknowns. For this, we are free to select $n - 1$ values of measurement errors. These are the allowable errors at the point P. If, instead of one performance parameter, we have k parameters, application of the above will yield a set of k nonlinear equations in n unknowns. If all partials for all equations are evaluated at the same point P, we can solve the system of equations simultaneously. However, if different points are used in evaluating the partials, then simultaneous solution of the system of equations must be viewed with caution.

Example 3.3

Problem Statement

The velocity of noncompressible fluid flow within a closed pipe (see process sketch below) can be quantified using Bernoulli's equation as

$$U = \left[2qg_c/\rho\right]^{\frac{1}{2}}$$

where q is dynamic pressure and is given by the following:

$$q = k(P_0 - P)$$

with P_0 defined as total pressure, P as static pressure, and k a calibration constant. Fluid density, ρ, is computed as:

$$\rho = P/R_G T$$

with R_G the universal gas constant, T the absolute static temperature, and g_c is the gravitational constant equal to 32.174 lbm ft/lbf sec^2. Establish the total measurement accuracy requirements in P_0, P, and T necessary to achieve an uncertainty in fluid velocity of less than 0.5 percent at the following conditions:

$$P_0 = 2050 \text{ psf}, \ P = 2000 \text{ psf}, \ T = 559.6° \text{ R}, \ R_G = 53.36 \ \frac{\text{ft lbf}}{°\text{R lbm}}$$

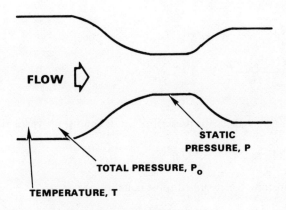

Process Sketch Illustrating Flow in a Closed Pipe

Solution

Rewriting Bernoulli's equation in terms of the measurements P_o, P, and T, we establish the following equation.

$$U = \left[(2k \, (P_0 - P) \, g_c)/(P/R_G T)\right]^{1/2}$$

Simplifying yields

$$U = \left[\frac{CT \, (P_0 - P)}{P}\right]^{1/2}$$

with C equal to $2 \, kg_c \, R_G$.

Expanding in a Taylor series yields

$$\delta U = \frac{\partial U}{\partial P_0} \, \Delta P_0 + \frac{\partial U}{\partial P} \, \Delta P + \frac{\partial U}{\partial T} \, \Delta T + R$$

where ΔP_0, ΔP, and ΔT are measurement errors, δU is the resultant error in velocity, and R is the remainder term assumed to be zero.
The partial derivatives above are defined as:

$$\frac{\partial U}{\partial P_0} = \frac{CT}{2UP}$$

$$\frac{\partial U}{\partial P} = -\frac{CTP_0}{2UP^2}$$

$$\frac{\partial U}{\partial T} = \frac{C(P_0 - P)}{2UP}$$

Evaluating the partials at the prescribed set of conditions yields the following:

$$U = 219.2 \text{ ft/sec}, \quad C = 3{,}433.6$$

where the constant k is assumed to be equal to one.

$$\frac{\partial U}{\partial P_0} = 2.19$$

$$\frac{\partial U}{\partial P} = -2.25$$

$$\frac{\partial U}{\partial T} = 0.2$$

Applying the RSS yields

$$\delta U = \left[(2.19)^2 \Delta P_0^2 + (-2.25)^2 \Delta P^2 + (0.2)^2 \Delta T^2\right]^{1/2}$$

$$\delta U = \left[4.8 \Delta P_0^2 + 5.1 \Delta P^2 + 0.04 \Delta T^2\right]^{1/2}$$

At this velocity, the specified 0.5 percent variation in U is 1.096. Using this and solving for the intersections yields the following maximum errors in the individual measurements.

Max ΔP_0 = 0.50 psf
Max ΔP = 0.48 psf
Max ΔT = 5.48 °F

Of these, the pressure errors are considered extremely stringent since they are approximately 0.02 percent of reading. It should be emphasized that the maximum individual errors listed above assume that there is no error in the other two measurements. Refer to Example 3.5 for further insight into the pressure measurement difficulties.

Example 3.4

Problem Statement

Solve the problem stated in Example 3.3 in metric rather than English units.

Solution

The equation defining velocity is the same with the exception that the gravitational constant g_c is not used. Thus,

$$U = [2q/\rho]^{1/2}$$

Dimensionally, the variables have the following form:

Variable	Dimension
U	m/sec
q	N/m^2
P_0	N/m^2
P	N/m^2
T	K
ρ	kg/m^3
R_G	287.1 J/kgK

Example 3.5

Problem Statement

In Example 3.3 separate transducers were used to measure the total and static pressures. Using this approach, it was shown that the pressure measurement accuracy requirements are stringent (e.g., accuracies of 0.2% of reading at the point considered). Rather than using separate transducers to measure both total and static pressure, use a differential pressure transducer configured to provide a direct measure of dynamic pressure.

Solution

The equation describing velocity is

$$U = [2qg_c/\rho]^{1/2}$$

with

$$\rho = P/R_G T$$

Thus, three measurements are required — P, T, and q. Rewriting yields:

$$U = \left[\frac{cqT}{P} \right]^{1/2}$$

with

$$c = 2g_c R_G$$

Expanding in a Taylor series yields:

$$\delta U = \frac{\partial U}{\partial q} \Delta q + \frac{\partial U}{\partial P} \Delta P + \frac{\partial U}{\partial T} \Delta T$$

where

$$\frac{\partial U}{\partial q} = \frac{cT}{2UP}$$

$$\frac{\partial U}{\partial P} = \frac{-cqT}{2UP^2}$$

$$\frac{\partial U}{\partial T} = \frac{cq}{2UP}$$

Evaluating the partials at the same conditions as Example 3.3 and applying the RSS yields:

$$\delta U = [4.8\Delta q^2 + 0.003\Delta P^2 + 0.04\Delta T^2]^{1/2}$$

Direct comparison of the coefficients of the measurement error coefficients indicates that the only change is the ΔP coefficient. Using the specified 0.5 percent variation in U and solving for the intersections yields the following maximum errors in the individual measurements:

Max. Δq = 0.5 psf
Max. ΔP = 20.0 psf
Max. ΔT = 5.48°F

Here, the allowable error in the q measurement is 0.5 psf, which is what we had computed for the ΔP_0 error in Example 3.3. While the magnitude is the same, the q measurement's range is significantly less. As a percent of reading, this error in q is 1 percent. The allowable error in the P measurement increased from 0.48 psf to 20 psf (a one percent of reading error). The error in T remained unchanged.

Example 3.6

Problem Statement

Some aerodynamic facilities that use air as a working fluid are used in applications intended to measure the heating or cooling efficiency of devices. For such applications, the device to be tested is mounted in the airstream and fluid from an external source is circulated through the device. By measuring both the temperature and mass of the fluid flowing into and out of the device, the amount of heat transferred to the facility's air stream can be computed. Similarly, the amount of heat added to or extracted from the facility's airstream can be computed by measuring both the airstream temperature differential and the mass of air flow. For such facilities, the device's heating/cooling efficiency is computed using both techniques.

Compute the measurement accuracy required to achieve an agreement between the two heat transfer techniques of one percent.

Solution

Consider the schematic arrangement shown below:

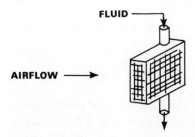

The heat transfer equation for the fluid flowing through the device is:

$$Q_w = \dot{m}_w \, Cp_w \, \Delta T_w$$

where

Q_w = heat loss (gain), Btu/sec
$\dot{m}_w$ = fluid mass flow, lbs/sec
Cp_w = fluid heat coefficient
ΔT_w = temperature difference across device, °F

Similarly, the heat transfer equation for the airstream side is:

$$Q_A = \dot{m}_A \, Cp_A \, \Delta T_A$$

Assuming that there are no external heat losses or gains and that all heat lost by the device is absorbed by the air, the one percent repeatability can be represented by the following equation:

$$0.99 \leq \frac{Q_A}{Q_W} \leq 1.01$$

Let

$$x = \frac{Q_A}{Q_W}$$

Then

$$x = \frac{\dot{m}_A \, C_{PA} \, \Delta T_A}{\dot{m}_w \, C_{PW} \, \Delta T_W}$$

$$x = k \, \frac{\dot{m}_A \, \Delta T_A}{\dot{m}_W \, \Delta T_W}$$

where

$$k = \frac{Cp_A}{Cp_W}$$

The measurements involved are the two mass flows and two temperature differentials. To establish the required measurement accuracy, it is necessary to examine sensitivities of x to variations in the different measurements. Expanding the above in a Taylor series yields:

$$\delta x = \frac{\partial x}{\partial \dot{m}_A} (\Delta \dot{m}_A) + \frac{\partial x}{\partial \Delta T_A} \Delta(\Delta T_A) + \frac{\partial x}{\partial \dot{m}_W} (\Delta \dot{m}_W) + \frac{\partial x}{\partial \Delta T_W} \Delta(\Delta T_W) + R$$

where $\Delta \dot{m}_A$, $\Delta(\Delta T_A)$, $\Delta \dot{m}_W$, and $\Delta(\Delta T_W)$ represent measurement errors.

Substituting for the partials and assuming $R = 0$ yields:

$$\delta x = \frac{x}{\dot{m}_A} (\Delta \dot{m}_A) + \frac{x}{\Delta T_A} \Delta(\Delta T_A) - \frac{x}{\dot{m}_W} (\Delta \dot{m}_W) - \frac{x}{\Delta T_W} \Delta(\Delta T_W)$$

Rearranging yields

$$\frac{\delta x}{x} = \frac{\Delta \dot{m}_A}{\dot{m}_A} + \frac{\Delta(\Delta T_A)}{\Delta T_A} - \frac{\Delta \dot{m}_W}{\dot{m}_W} - \frac{\Delta(\Delta T_W)}{\Delta T_W}$$

Since the measurement errors are random variables, some error cancellation will occur. Applying the RSS yields:

$$\left(\frac{\delta x}{x}\right)^2 = \left(\frac{\Delta \dot{m}_A}{\dot{m}_A}\right)^2 + \left(\frac{\Delta(\Delta T_A)}{\Delta T_A}\right)^2 + \left(\frac{\Delta \dot{m}_W}{\dot{m}_W}\right)^2 + \left(\frac{\Delta(\Delta T_W)}{\Delta T_W}\right)^2$$

Assuming the errors are equally divided among the four sources, then the one percent criteria can be achieved if each parameter is measured to a 0.5 percent accuracy.

3.3 INTERPRETATION OF SOLUTION

Application of the above technique will produce allowable variations for each measurement at the point P. That is, given global performance criteria δF_i, we establish the following corresponding limits for Δm_m:

$$\left| \Delta m_m \right| \leq C_m \tag{3.10}$$

If we repeat this at other points, we can establish for each measurement m_m the allowable variations at different points within the measurement range (Figure 3.2).

As shown, we have established errors at multiple points within the range and have presented these both in terms of allowable variations and in percent of reading. The presentation is of interest in that it may imply that a single measurement may not exhibit the required variation characteristics over the complete range. This is especially true since manufacturer's specifications are generally stated in terms of percent of full scale and not percent of reading.

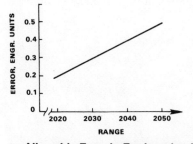

a. Allowable Error in Engineering Units

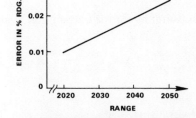

b. Allowable Error in % Reading

Figure 3.2. Allowable Measurement Variation Characteristics Over the Range of Interest

Thus, we may be required to subdivide the measurement into several measurements, each of which has a range that is a subset of the total required range.

Since we know that the computed measurement variation will consist of both fixed and random components, the measurement variations we have established at each point can be viewed as measurement uncertainty intervals. Thus, we have:

$$-C_m \leq \Delta m_m \leq C_m \tag{3.11}$$

In light of the probabilistic nature of errors, we must attach a confidence level to this interval. The confidence interval we use must be based on the global performance parameter criteria δF_i. For example, if we want to ensure that 95 percent of the time the uncertainty in F_i is less than δF_i, we would attach a 95 percent confidence level to the different Δm_m intervals.

3.4 BASIS FOR DESIGN

3.4.1 Significance of Error Propagation

As we stated, measurements are made for the principal purpose of producing information. Since decisions are made based on that information and since we know that every measurement is in error, it is essential that we quantify the goodness of the information. That is, we know that there is some uncertainty associated with the information that is attributable to measurement error. Consequently, decisions must be based not on absolute values of information but rather on confidence intervals. If we already have an existing system, we can design and conduct an experiment that we can use to establish the uncertainty interval. With this approach, any information produced would have an uncertainty associated with it that had been determined experimentally.

As an example of the significance of this confidence interval concept, consider a research and development program for widgets, where the performance of the widget is defined by the parameter F, which can be represented as

$$F = f(m_1, m_2, \ldots, m_n) \tag{3.12}$$

where the m_i are measurements. From our previous discussions, we know that there are errors associated with each measurement and thus there is an uncertainty with F of δF that is based on a desired confidence level of $1 - \alpha$. If we want to determine whether or not a change in the widget design significantly affects performance, we make the change, repeat the measurements, compute a value for the performance parameter of say F', and compare this to the value of the performance parameter (F_0) before the change. The question we must answer is whether the difference between F' and F_0 is significant. If the difference $(F' - F_0)$ is less than the uncertainty in F of δF, we are confident to a level of $1 - \alpha$ that the change is not significant. Conversely, there is a probability of α that the change is significant but will go undetected. The consequence of erroneous decisions are the basis by which the confidence level $1 - \alpha$ should be established.

The error propagation technique provides a mechanism whereby the uncertainty interval for a performance parameter, $F = f(m_1, m_2, \ldots, m_n)$, can be established based on the error associated with each individual measurement Δm_n. This is important in that if we have an existing system, we can perform an experiment and use this error propagation technique to determine the parameter uncertainty. However, the real significance of this approach is that error propagation represents the basis for a measurement system design technique. That is, we begin the process by asking the following fundamental questions:

- What information is required?
- How good must this information be?

We then use this to establish the required individual measurement error requirements Δm_n. If the system is designed and built to satisfy these individual measurement error specifications, we can be assured that the uncertainty associated with the information to be produced will be acceptable to a desired confidence level of $1 - \alpha$.

3.4.2 Establishing Subsystem Error Budgets Based on Δm_m

The individual measurement error requirements, Δm_m, which we have established based on the performance parameter criteria δF_i, represent total measurement error. We know, however, that the system we use to measure m_m will consist of several subsystems. That is, we will have sensors, probes, signal conditioners, etc. Each of these subsystems will exhibit error characteristics that, for the total m_m measurement chain, will combine to produce Δm_m. Since their combined error must be less than the computed total measurement error, it is of interest from a designer's point of view to determine if there is a way of systematically budgeting errors for each subsystem based on Δm_m. If so, this would provide sound subsystem selection criteria based on total system performance.

Consider the measurement system shown in Figure 3.3. As shown, the system consists of various elements, each of which introduces an error e_i in the measurement chain. The total measurement error, Δm_m, is a function of the individual elemental errors e_i. That is,

$$\Delta m_m = f(e_i) \tag{3.13}$$

We postulate that each element has a normal error distribution and use the RSS technique to estimate total measurement error Δm_m as

$$\Delta m_m = \pm \ (B_m + t_\alpha S_m) \tag{3.14}$$

$$B_m = \left[B_1^2 + B_2^2 + \ldots + B_n^2 \right]^{\frac{1}{2}} \tag{3.15}$$

$$S_m = \left[S_1^2 + S_2^2 + \ldots + S_n^2 \right]^{\frac{1}{2}} \tag{3.16}$$

and t_α is selected using the Student T table based on desired confidence $1 - \alpha$.

If we have an existing system, we can quantify the total measurement error, Δm_m, by conducting an experiment. Ideally, we would design an experiment that would test the entire measurement chain rather than each element. Thus, we would not be concerned with quantifying each elemental error e_i but rather with the total error. In the design mode, we do not have a system. Instead, we have a specification for total measurement error, Δm_m, and are thus interested in specifying the performance of individual pieces of equipment such that when integrated they will exhibit a total measurement error of Δm_m. That is, we want to distribute the total measurement error to the different system elements for measurement m_m such that when combined they will provide an estimate of total error that is less than or equal to Δm_m.

Budgeting is a process whereby we distribute total measurement error to the different elements based on engineering judgment as to what is realizable and available in the marketplace. If we assume that total measurement error for the system of Figure 3.3 can be approximated as

$$\Delta m_m^2 = e_1^2 + e_2^2 + \ldots + e_8^2 \tag{3.17}$$

where no distinction is made between fixed and random error, then we can group terms as

$$\Delta m_m^2 = (e_1^2 + e_2^2) + (e_3^2 + \ldots + e_8^2) \tag{3.18}$$

Note that this can be restated as:

$$\text{Total Meas Error} = \left[(\text{Sensor Errors})^2 + (\text{Data System Errors})^2 \right]^{\frac{1}{2}} \tag{3.19}$$

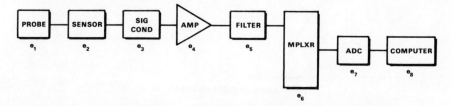

Figure 3.3. Measurement System Chain with Elemental Errors

Figure 3.4 is a graphical representation of the RSS quadratic relationship. For simplicity, we have restricted the presentation to a circular relationship in the first quadrant. As shown, the radius is equal to the total measurement error. We can use this graphical representation as a design aid by specifying the error component we wish to budget (either the sensor errors or data system errors) and then solving for the other. For example, we may decide based on knowledge of available data systems that the error budget for the data system should have a value of a. This automatically implies that the sensor errors must be less than or equal to b if the total measurement error specification is to be satisfied. Using the value budgeted for sensor errors of b, we can construct another relationship as

$$\text{Sensor Errors}^2 = e_1^2 + e_2^2 = b^2 \tag{3.20}$$

This can be used to establish a budget for the sensor and for the probe. Similarly, the value we budgeted for the data system can be used to create another relationship as

$$\text{Data System Errors}^2 = e_3^2 + \ldots + e_8^2 = a^2 \tag{3.21}$$

We would logically group the elements e_3 to e_8 into two elements and establish a budget for each group. This binary decomposition would continue until we had established a budget value for each elemental error.

In general, we have n subsystems and thus the total measurement error relationship is given by:

$$\Delta m_m = \left[e_1^2 + e_2^2 + \ldots + e_n^2 \right]^{1/2} \tag{3.22}$$

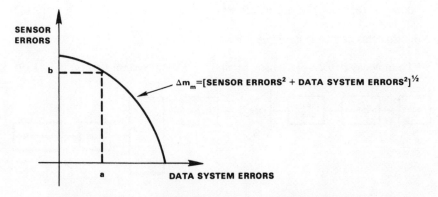

Figure 3.4. The RSS Depicted as a Circular Relationship

For this, we can let

$$E_{1,1}^2 = e_1^2 + e_2^2 + \ldots + e_k^2 \tag{3.23}$$

and

$$E_{2,1}^2 = e_{k+1}^2 + e_{k+2}^2 + \ldots + e_n^2 \tag{3.24}$$

Substituting we get

$$\Delta m_m = \left[E_{1,1}^2 + E_{1,2}^2 \right]^{1/2} \tag{3.25}$$

If we select values to satisfy the relationship for $E_{1,1}$ and $E_{1,2}$ of C_1 and C_2, then we have the following two relationships:

$$E_{1,1}^2 = e_1^2 + e_2^2 + \ldots + e_k^2 = C_1^2 \tag{3.26}$$

$$E_{2,1}^2 = e_{k+1}^2 + e_{k+2}^2 + \ldots + e_n^2 = C_2^2 \tag{3.27}$$

For each of these, we can further decompose into two elements. For example, the relationship

$$E_{1,1}^2 = e_1^2 + e_2^2 + \ldots + e_k^2 = C_1^2 \tag{3.28}$$

can be decomposed into

$$C_1^2 = E_{1,2}^2 + E_{1,3}^2 \tag{3.29}$$

where

$$E_{1,2}^2 = e_1^2 + e_2^2 + \ldots + e_l^2 \tag{3.30}$$

and

$$E_{1,3}^2 = e_{l+1}^2 + e_{l+2}^2 + \ldots + e_k^2 \tag{3.31}$$

We can construct a circle of radius C_1 and use this to budget errors for $E_{1,2}$ and $E_{1,3}$. This binary decomposition process can be extended until we have established a budget for each elemental error. Figure 3.5 illustrates the graphical representation of this binary decomposition process.

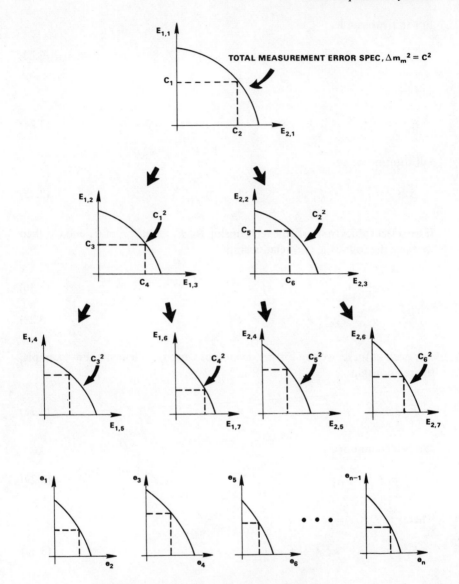

**Figure 3.5. Establishing Elemental Error Budgets
Based on Global Specifications**

3.5 SUMMARY

In this chapter, we have illustrated that informational relationships and specifications for the goodness of these can be used in conjunction with error propagation techniques to establish specifications for total measurement error. These individual total measurement specifications can then be used to establish error budgets for each system element. If we select equipment based on specifications derived in this manner, we will be assured that the total measurement error specification will be realized and that the specified goodness of the information parameter will be realized.

Error budgeting requires knowledge of the types of magnitudes of errors that may be encountered for each element of a measurement chain. Once identified, we then use manufacturer's published specifications to quantify each of the errors. In the following chapter, we review the fundamentals of data systems before we establish error models for some of the more common types of measurements. These provide (1) a method for comparing the performance of different configurations and (2) estimates of the magnitudes of errors that we can use when establishing budgets.

Chapter 4
Sampled Data Systems

4.1 FUNDAMENTALS

4.1.1 Introduction

A data system can be considered to be the interface between the process with its measurement sensors and the observer. Consider Figure 4.1 where the process is equipped with n different sensors. The sensors may be used to measure pressure, temperature, flow, and position, and in general can be considered to be passive. The data system's primary functions are to support the sensor and to convert each sensor's output into a format presentable to the observer. The output may be an analog meter, a chart recorder, a magnetic tape recorder, and a digital display. Although data systems take on different forms, this chapter treats only multi-channel sampled data systems.

In general, a digital sampled data system consists of various components designed to support different types of sensors and provide an output compatible with a digital computer. Figure 4.2 illustrates a typical sampled data system that uses an amplifier-per-channel. As shown, several of the system's components are used to condition the sensor's output, while others are used to convert the analog signals to a digital format. While many variations of this system exist, the indicated arrangement is considered to be typical of high level multiplexed systems.

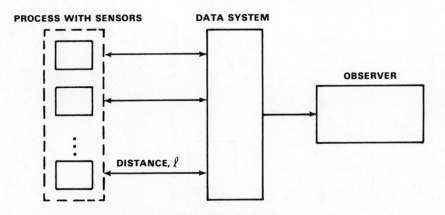

**Figure 4.1. Data System As the Interface
Between Process and Observer**

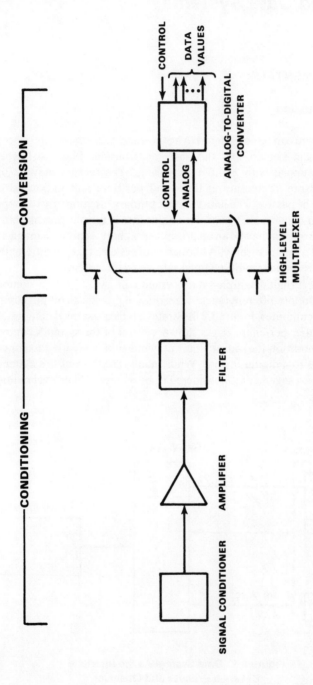

Figure 4.2. Sampled Data System Block Diagram

Our concern in this chapter is to develop techniques that can be used to systematically select the various system components that comprise the data system. Since we have focused on measurement accuracy and response, we specifically want to examine the data system to determine its measurement characteristics; that is, what system components affect total measurement accuracy and response and how significant are these effects.

4.1.2 Accuracy

For a digital system, one of the fundamental error concerns is the transition from a continuous analog signal to a set of discrete digital values that accurately represent the analog signal. For example, if we have an analog signal whose magnitude is A, then we must be concerned with what set of digital values accurately represent A. Assuming that n binary digital values (bits) are representative, where each bit has two distinct states (logic '0' or '1'), then the smallest analog signal we could indicate with an n-bit code is $A/2^n$. Thus, for any analog signal we represent with this code, there is a potential error in the digital representation of $1/2\ (A/2^n)$. This error is called **quantizing error** and is the result of a transformation from the continuous analog to discrete digital.

There are many other error sources in addition to quantization. Typically these include linearity, hysteresis, thermal induced offset and sensitivity, noise, cross talk, and loading. Each system component must be considered and the errors quantified before an estimate of the total system accuracy can be made.

4.1.3 Response

To establish the data system response requirements, it is necessary to first establish what is required to characterize the process. Consider Figure 4.3a where the time history of all process measurements can be considered relatively invariant. For such a case, one measurement per parameter is adequate with the process state being characterized by a single set of measurements taken anywhere in time. Since the process measurements are relatively constant, the data system response requirements are not critical.

In contrast to the time-invariant process shown in Figure 4.3a, consider Figure 4.3b where the amplitude is seen to vary with time. For such a case, a single measurement sample is not adequate to describe the process. For any one process signal, several discrete samples are required to reconstruct the continuous signal. Consequently, both the number of samples and the time between samples for any one process signal are of fundamental importance.

In addition to the concern over the number of samples and the sampling rate required to characterize a system input, consideration must be given to the dynamic parameters of the system components. If the inputs are changing rapidly, care must be taken in selecting components to ensure that their dynamic characteristics are consistent.

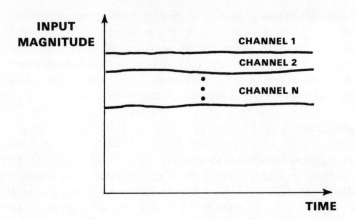

a. Typical Time History of Stationary Process

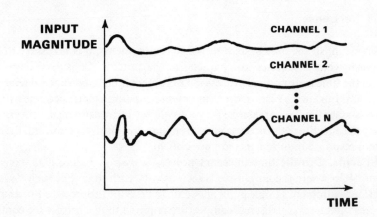

b. Typical Time History of Dynamic Process

**Figure 4.3. Typical Time History of Stationary
and Dynamic Processes**

4.1.4 Design Approach

Before we can effectively design a sampled data system, it is necessary to examine the different components and their functions. While there is a wide variety of sampled data systems, the common requirements are to condition signals and to convert them into a digital format. For multichannel systems, hardware multiplexing is generally used because of economic advantages of time sharing equipment. The remainder of this chapter is devoted to a cursory look at the components and techniques under headings of signal conditioning, multiplexing, and signal conversion.

4.2 SIGNAL CONDITIONING

Signal conditioning is a broad term with various connotations. Since we have stated that the primary functions of a sampled data system are to condition and convert signals, we seek to define signal conditioning accordingly. When viewed in this context, a signal conditioner can be defined as the interface between the sensor and the converter. As such, the signal conditioner must perform the following functions:

1. Provide sensor excitation
2. Compensate for signal offsets
3. Provide system and sensor calibration
4. Provide amplification of the input signal to match converter input requirements
5. Accommodate differences in zero potential references
6. Limit signal bandwidth

To provide these functions, various electronic assemblies are used. For example, items 1-3 are normally provided by a unit called a signal conditioner, items 4-5 by an amplifier, and item 6 by a filter. In practice, the units may be packaged as one assembly or as several different pieces of equipment. Here, we functionally separate signal conditioning into three units for discussion only.

4.3 SIGNAL CONDITIONERS

4.3.1 Excitation

Since most sensors are passive — i.e., they require a source of excitation — the signal conditioner must provide sensor excitation. Generally, this takes the form of a precise, well-regulated dc voltage or current. There are, however, some solid state sensors that have internal regulators and require only 24–28 V dc excitation. To compensate for differences in lead wire resistance, remote sensing of the sensor excitation is usually performed. A power supply used for this function should have constant voltage or constant current capabilities, remote sensing, current limiting to protect the sensor, good stability, minimal noise, and be easily adjustable.

4.3.2 Compensation

While it can be argued that hardware compensation for signal offsets is not necessary with today's computer-based systems, there is still a need to scale the converter's input to achieve maximum resolution. If the sensor has a significant offset, the amplifier gain is restricted, which limits the resolution of the conversion of the signal of real interest. Consequently, some degree of compensation for signal offsets is required. To illustrate the principle of offset compensation, consider the two common methods used to balance strain gage transducers shown in Figure 4.4.

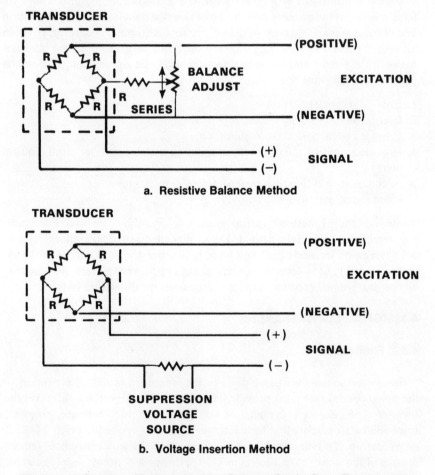

Figure 4.4. Common Methods Used to Balance Strain Gage Transducers

The most common technique of bridge balancing is the resistive balance network, which functions by applying a shunt across two adjacent arms. When the balance potentiometer is in the exact center, equal shunts are applied across each of the two arms, which results in no change in the output. However, when the balance potentiometer is moved from the center position, unequal shunts are applied to the two arms, which affects the bridge output, thereby providing a means of adjustment. While the shunt balancing technique provides a means of compensating for unwanted outputs, it does affect the transducer sensitivity by loading the bridge arms. The maximum loading effect in percent of full scale is:

$$\text{Max Loading} = -R/(4\,R_{series}) \times 100 \tag{4.1}$$

where R is the bridge arm resistance, and R_{series} is the series resistance in the balance potentiometer wiper. To reduce the loading effects, R_{series} should be much greater than the bridge arm resistance. However, the size of R_{series} affects the adjustment range according to the following equation:

$$\text{Balance Range} = \pm\,\text{Max Loading}/\text{F.S. Sensitivity} \tag{4.2}$$

where Max Loading is defined above, F.S. Sensitivity is the bridge full scale sensitivity expressed in mV/V, and Balance Range is expressed in percent of full scale. Hence, for minimum loading, only the required range of balance should be used with R_{series} as large as possible. Typical values of R_{series} are 40–50 kΩ when R is 300–1000 ohms.

The second common method for suppression is the voltage insertion technique. With this technique, an equal but opposing voltage is developed across a resistor placed in series with the bridge signal output. While this technique does not load the bridge as does the resistive balancing method, it does produce some complications. Since the suppression voltage is algebraically added to the bridge output voltage, any variations in the suppression voltage source are seen as variations in the bridge output. Hence, the suppression voltage source must not only be a highly stable device, but it must introduce little or no noise. Consequently, some techniques develop the suppression voltage excitation from the bridge excitation, while others use a separate stable power source.

4.3.3 Calibration

In addition to providing sensor excitation and compensating for signal offsets, signal conditioners generally include calibration provisions. If the sensor is a strain gage, a popular method of simulating a calibration is with resistive shunts. With this technique, a precision resistor located within the signal conditioner is placed in parallel across a bridge arm. Usually, low resistance devices such as relays are used to switch the calibration resistor across one or more bridge arms. Figure 4.5 illustrates a configuration where each of the bridge arms can be sequentially shunted with a single precision resistor. This technique uses a 10-wire system where four leads are used for shunt calibration, two for remote excitation sense, and four for the normal sensor hookup. There are several variations that use from 6 to 10 wires to accommodate the necessary functions.

In addition to providing a means to simulate strain gage transducer outputs, the signal conditioner is often configured in such a manner that a signal conditioner's input can be disconnected from the sensor and reconnected to an external precision voltage source. This technique permits end-to-end calibration of the data system. For a multichannel system, it is standard practice to connect all signal conditioner calibrate inputs to a common bus. This is shown in Figure 4.6. In some cases, it may be possible to calibrate all channels simultaneously using a single voltage source. Proper precaution should be taken to ensure that an overload or defective channel does not affect the remaining channels.

4.4 AMPLIFIER

4.4.1 General

The amplifier's basic functions are to scale the converter's inputs and to accommodate differences in zero potential, which may exist between the sensor and the data system. Since the converters have fixed ranges (typically ±5 V,

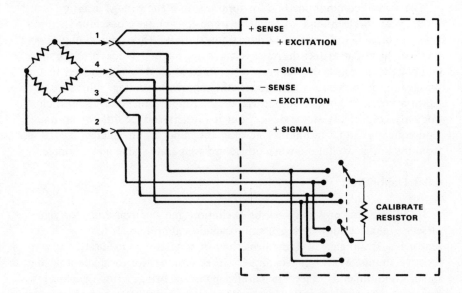

Figure 4.5. Resistive Calibration Using 10-Wire System

±10 V), it is desirable to take advantage of the converter's resolution by appropriately scaling the input. To accomplish this, either a single-ended or a differential amplifier is used. If there is a difference in the zero potential between the sensor and the data system, a differential amplifier, which effectively isolates the sensor and converter reference points, is preferred. Even with this approach, there are problems and potential error sources as noted in the following paragraphs.

4.4.2 Common Mode

An often overlooked error source results from common mode voltage. Since measurement sensors are generally remotely located from the data system, it is

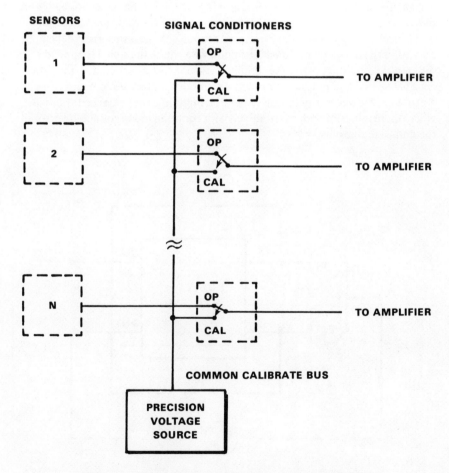

Figure 4.6. Multichannel Calibration Using Common Bus

highly likely that the signals are developed in a zero potential region that differs from the zero potential of the data system. The difference in zero potential between the two areas can result in a voltage being developed in each of the two signal leads, as illustrated in Figure 4.7. If the voltage at each input is measured with respect to the data system reference potential, a voltage whose magnitude is greater than the signal source (E_{s1} or E_{s2}) will be observed. This is defined as **common mode voltage**.

Common mode voltage can create two major problems. First of all, if the voltage is of sufficient magnitude, it can damage the data system. Because most data systems are solid-state electronic devices, common mode voltages exceeding the system's power supply (typically ± 15 V) can destroy an input stage. For some chemical and industrial processes, common mode voltages often exceed this. Consequently, the data system to which these signals are input must be designed accordingly. For applications where the common mode voltage is on the order of a few volts, the data system input requires no special attention.

The second major problem of common mode voltage is the error that can be created in the data signal. Consider Figure 4.8a where the signal is applied to a differential amplifier. Since the amplifier output is proportional to the difference between the signal leads, the common mode voltage does not appear to be a problem. However, this is true only if the input lines are balanced. For cases where there is line imbalance combined with common mode voltage, an error in the data signal results.

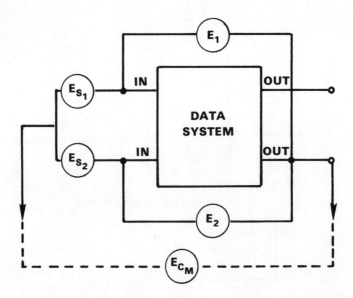

Figure 4.7. Common Mode Voltage Resulting From Earth Potential Differences

The error is a result of common mode voltage being converted to normal-mode voltage through unequal impedances. Consider Figure 4.8b where the circuit has been redrawn. Here the common mode voltage is shown as the bridge excitation with the bridge output being the normal mode voltage. The resistances R_1 and R_2 are the lumped line and transducer resistances. The impedances Z_1 and Z_2 are leakage impedances and are considered to be capacitive. The ratio of E_C to E_N is defined as the common mode rejection ratio (CMRR), which is a measure of the amplifier's ability to reject the presence of common mode voltage. Note that CMRR can be increased by increasing the leakage impedance and/or balancing the signal lines.

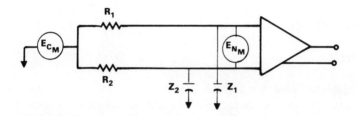

a. Common Mode Voltage Converted to Normal Mode Voltage

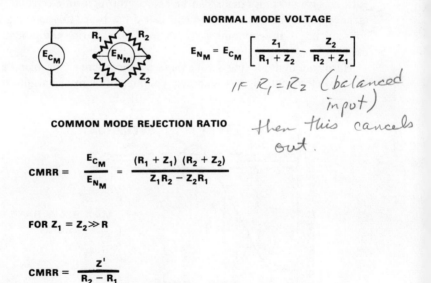

NORMAL MODE VOLTAGE

$$E_{N_M} = E_{C_M} \left[\frac{z_1}{R_1 + Z_2} - \frac{z_2}{R_2 + Z_1} \right]$$

IF $R_1 = R_2$ (balanced input) then this cancels out.

COMMON MODE REJECTION RATIO

$$CMRR = \frac{E_{C_M}}{E_{N_M}} = \frac{(R_1 + Z_1)(R_2 + Z_2)}{Z_1 R_2 - Z_2 R_1}$$

FOR $Z_1 = Z_2 \gg R$

$$CMRR = \frac{z'}{R_2 - R_1}$$

b. Equivalent Bridge Circuit

Figure 4.8. Error Signal Resulting From Common Mode Voltage

4.4.3 Dynamic and Static Errors

If the input data are dynamic, consideration must be given to the amplifier's ability to respond to a rapidly changing input. Of special concern are the amplifier's settling time and slew rate specifications. If a step function is applied to an amplifier's input as shown in Figure 4.9, a finite time is required for the amplifier's output to settle to within a specified tolerance band. Also shown is the graphical interpretation of slew rate, which is a measure of the amplifier's ability to accurately track the rate of change of input signals. In addition to the dynamic parameters, consideration must be given to the static parameters (linearity, gain accuracy, stability, hysteresis, and noise) in selecting an amplifier.

4.5 MULTIPLEXERS

4.5.1 General

For applications involving multiple measurements, the data system functional requirements are signal conditioning and digital conversion for each measurement. For multi-channel systems, this requires either duplicating expensive equipment for each measurement or resorting to a technique where various system components can be shared through an electronic switching arrangement. This latter technique is called **hardware multiplexing** and, as a consequence of the economic advantages of time sharing equipment, is widely used.

Hardware multiplexing is not a panacea since there are problems associated with switching data signals. The close coupling of many signals produces cross

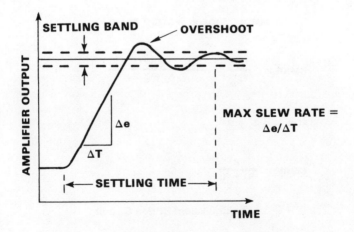

Figure 4.9. Amplifier Response to a Step Input

talk between the various channels, which affects the measurement accuracy. The switch itself must be viewed as having a certain transfer accuracy that is a function of source impedance, switch resistance, frequency, and thermal induced voltages. Additionally, there is a finite settling time required for the switch to activate and for the signal to settle to some specified tolerance. Even with such problems, the economic advantages are such that multiplexing is widely used today in data systems.

Figure 4.10a illustrates a multichannel system where each channel has identical equipment components. That is, each channel has both signal conditioning and digital conversion equipment. One means of reducing equipment cost would be to time share all equipment as shown in Figure 4.10b. Since most sensors produce signals in the millivolt range, this technique is called low level multiplexing. Since there are technical problems and limitations with switching low level signals, amplifiers are often used before the switching device, resulting in high level multiplexing, as shown in Figure 4.10c. While the amplifier-per-channel technique is more expensive than the low level multiplexing technique, many of the problems associated with switching low level signals are either eliminated or significantly reduced with high level multiplexing.

4.5.2 Low Level Multiplexing

Figure 4.11a illustrates a system that employs the low level multiplexing technique. Here, a number of low level signals time share a differential amplifier and an analog-to-digital converter using electromechanical switches. Since the signals are low level, it is necessary to maintain a continuous signal guard through the switch to the amplifier to minimize noise. Significant problems associated with this technique in addition to signal guarding are:

- Thermal-induced voltages
- Cross talk
- Speed
- Channel-to-channel interference

An additional problem is that the sampling rate is required to be higher to achieve a specified level of distortion resulting from frequency folding. Since the signals are low level, passive filters are generally used for anti-aliasing. Because such filters have at most two poles, it is generally not possible to achieve the filter characteristics necessary to minimize frequency folding distortion. Typical throughput for an electromechanical multiplexer is 200 channels/second.

Another popular technique of multiplexing low level signals uses a capacitive transfer technique. Figure 4.11 illustrates the multiplexer arrangement called a flying capacitor multiplexer. With this technique, a capacitor is connected across the signal source and is used to transfer the signal from the source to the input amplifier. When a channel is selected, the source is disconnected and the capacitor connected to the amplifier. The flying capacitor technique does have advantages in that it can accommodate high common mode voltages, is both

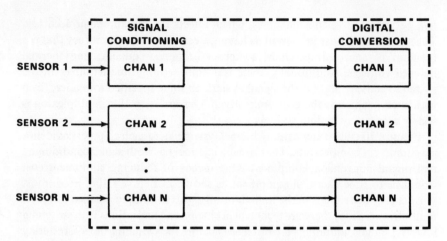

a. Multichannel System with Replicated Equipment

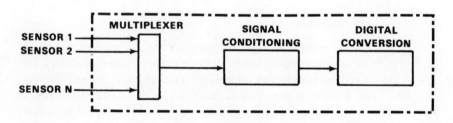

b. Low Level Multiplexing Technique

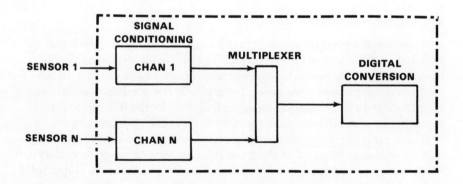

c. High Level Multiplexing Technique

Figure 4.10. Muiltichannel Data System Arrangements

simple and economical, and offers good noise rejection. The major disadvantage is that large capacitances are required, which, when combined with the source resistance, forms a simple filter that limits the bandwidth to a few hertz. Typical throughput rates are 200 channels/second.

4.5.3 High Level Multiplexing

If an amplifier is used with each channel prior to the multiplexer, as shown in Figure 4.12, several significant advantages can be realized. Problems associated with switching guard shields, as well as that of generating thermal voltages with the switching technique, are virtually eliminated. With high level signals, high

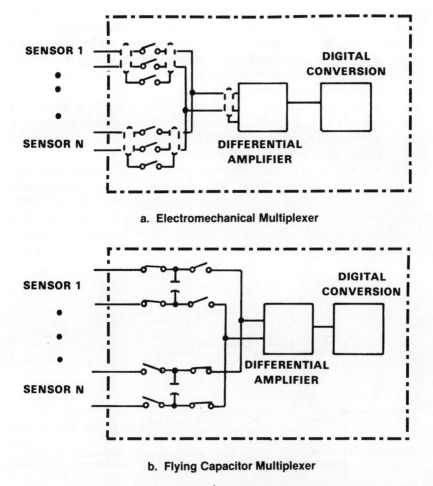

a. Electromechanical Multiplexer

b. Flying Capacitor Multiplexer

Figure 4.11. Low Level Multiplexing Techniques

speed solid state switches can be used as the multiplexer, yielding throughput rates of several hundred thousand channels/second. Additionally, active filters having several poles can be used, which reduces the required sampling rate necessary to achieve a specified level of frequency folding distortion. The significant disadvantage is the equipment cost.

4.6 ANALOG-TO-DIGITAL CONVERSION

4.6.1 Quantization

The heart of the sampled data system is the analog-to-digital converter. Here, a transition is made from a continuous analog variable to a discrete digital code. The conversion process, which is termed quantization, presents a potentially large error source to the designer. Since a finite number is being used to represent a continuum, there is an uncertainty associated with the code representation that is a function of the maximum finite number size. For example, if an analog signal that varies between zero and ten volts is to be converted using a 3-bit converter, all bits being logically true can be used to represent ten volts, and all bits logically false can be used to represent zero volts. Since each bit has two states (true and false), there are eight different possibilities that can be represented with a 3-bit code. For this example, we can resolve a ten-volt signal into eight parts. The resolution is then 10/8 or 1.25 volts. The magnitude of this error is a function of the number of bits used.

Consider Figure 4.13, which illustrates the quantization error for a 3-bit converter. Since there are eight possible codes, a decision must be made as to which code to use. The customary practice is to divide the input range into n equal sized segments, where n is the number of unique code possibilities, and to place the decision level at the midpoints of the segments. For the 3-bit converter, the segment sizes are 1.25 volts with decision points at 0.625 V, 1.875 V, 3.125 V,

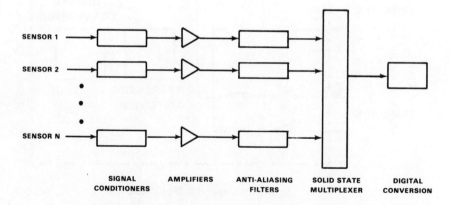

Figure 4.12. High Level Multiplexing Data System

etc. If the input voltage is between zero and 0.625 V, a code of 000 is used to represent the variable. For an input from 0.625 V to 1.875 V, a code of 001 is used.

As shown in Figure 4.13, the quantizer error is $\pm\frac{1}{2}$ LSB, where LSB is the value of the least significant bit. For the 3-bit converter example, the LSB has the value of 1.25 volts. As shown, the error function has a sawtooth characteristic and is zero only at the decision level midpoints. The magnitude of this error can be reduced only by increasing the number of bits. Table 4.1 lists the relationship between the number of bits, the number of states, and the value of the LSB. The quantization error for a 12-bit converter would be ± 0.000122, or ± 0.01 percent of full scale. Similarly, a 10-bit converter has a quantization error of approximately ± 0.05 percent of full scale.

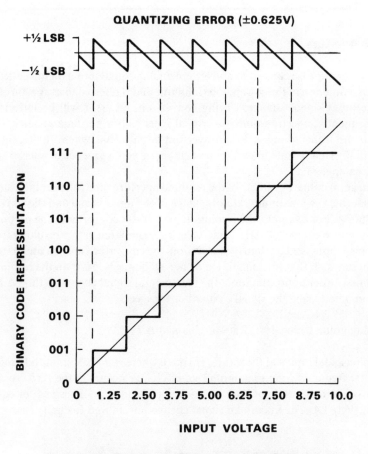

Figure 4.13. Quantization Error for a 3-Bit Converter

Table 4.1. Relationship Between Number of Bits and LSB

NUMBER OF BITS n	NUMBER OF STATES 2^n	VALUE OF LSB 2^{-n}
8	256	3.91×10^{-3}
9	512	1.95×10^{-3}
10	1024	9.77×10^{-4}
11	2048	4.88×10^{-4}
12	4096	2.44×10^{-4}
13	8192	1.22×10^{-4}
14	16384	6.10×10^{-5}
15	32768	3.05×10^{-5}
16	65536	1.53×10^{-5}

4.6.2 Aperture

A finite time is required to convert an analog signal into a digital code. The time is a function of the conversion technique and is referred to as **aperture time**. If the input signal changes during conversion, an error will be introduced. Consequently, aperture time is a critical specification for data systems whose inputs are nonstationary. For conversion applications where the signals are essentially steady state, measurement errors as a consequence of aperture time are meaningless.

An approximate estimate of the required aperture time can be established by considering the maximum rate-of-change of the input signal and the converter resolution. For example, the resolution for a 10-bit converter is one part out of 2^{10}, or approximately 0.001 of full scale. To ensure that errors resulting from a changing input are less than the resolution, the converter's aperture time should be chosen such that the magnitude of signal change is less than the resolution. To a first-order approximation, the incremental signal change in time ΔT can be computed using the signal's rate-of-change as:

$$\text{Magnitude Change} = (\text{Rate-of-Change}) \, \Delta T \tag{4.3}$$

For sinusoidal inputs of the form $A \sin(\omega t)$, where A is peak amplitude and ω is angular frequency, the maximum rate-of-change occurs at the zero crossover points. The magnitude of the rate-of-change at these points is ωA, or equivalently $(2\pi f)A$. The maximum signal change normalized for unity is:

$$\text{Max Signal Change} = \frac{(2\pi f)A}{2A} = \pi f \tag{4.4}$$

The required aperture time, ΔT, can then be computed for a sinusoidal input as:

$$\Delta T = \frac{\text{Converter Resolution}}{\text{Max Signal Change}} = \frac{0.001}{\pi f} \text{ for a 10-bit converter} \quad (4.5)$$

For this example where f is 1 kHz and the converter is 10-bits, the aperture time is:

$$\Delta T = \frac{0.001}{(\pi)(1,000)} = 318 \times 10^{-9} \text{ seconds} \quad (4.6)$$

That is, the 10-bit converter must have an aperture time of 318 nanoseconds to ensure that errors resulting from a 1 kHz sinusodial signal are less than the resolution.

The above example illustrates the need for rapid conversion when the inputs are dynamic. However, these speeds are not generally achievable. Consequently, sample-and-hold devices are used to instantaneously sample a dynamic signal and hold it for conversion. These devices usually use a high quality capacitor with minimal leakage to store the signal for conversion. With this technique, the converter's aperture time is less critical. However, a finite time is required to charge the capacitor. That is, the sample-and-hold circuit also has an aperture time specification that must satisfy the aperture time criterion computed above. Figure 4.14 illustrates the required aperture time to maintain the error less than resolution for sinusoidal signals whose peak-to-peak amplitude equals the converter full scale range.

4.6.3 Successive Approximation Converter

One of the two most commonly used converters is the successive approximation converter. This device utilizes a technique whereby an analog input voltage, whose magnitude is unknown, is compared to precise fractional parts of an analog reference voltage in sequential programmed steps. At the completion of this conversion process, a digital word — whose elements represent the equivalent fractional parts — is formed.

Consider Figure 4.15a, which illustrates in block diagram form the functional components of a successive approximation converter. The unknown analog voltage is input to an operational amplifier configured as a comparator where a comparison is made to a precise reference voltage. The comparator's output, which is either logically true or false, indicates the relative magnitude between the input and a precise reference voltage. That is, the comparator may indicate logic true as long as the unknown voltage is greater than the reference and logic false whenever the unknown voltage is less than the reference. The comparator's output is then used in the control logic circuitry as a decision

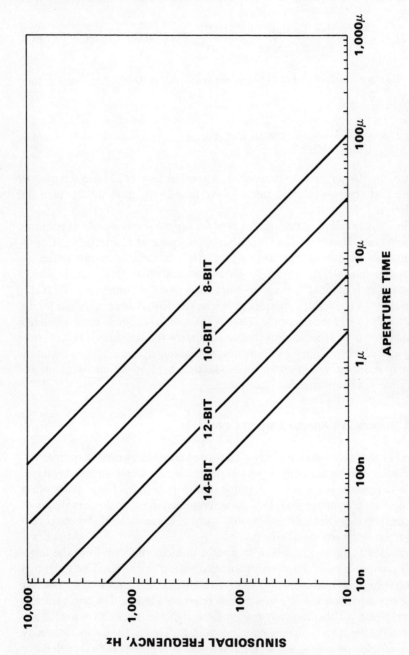

Figure 4.14. Required Aperture Time to Maintain Error
Less Than Resolution for Sinusoidal Inputs

device. If the reference is still less than the unknown voltage, the last incremental . weight is maintained and the reference is increased for a new comparison. If the reference is greater than the unknown voltage, the reference is decreased and the last incremental weight discarded.

Figure 4.15b illustrates the conversion process. At the start of conversion, the input is compared to the most significant bit, which corresponds to one-half of the converter's full scale analog input capability. If this is less than the unknown input, the converter's output bit is set logically true and the reference voltage is increased by the value of the next smaller bit. The reference would now be equal to one-half plus one-fourth full scale. Again the comparison is made. At this time, the reference exceeds the unknown voltage. Consequently, the second bit would be set logically false. The reference would now be increased by the value of the third bit and would equal one-half (bit 1) plus one-eighth (bit 3) full scale. As shown, the process would be repeated until all bits had been tested. Upon completion, the output register would contain either logic true ('1') or false ('0') for each of the converter's n bits.

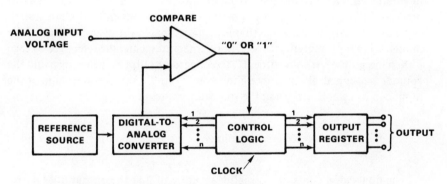

a. Functional Components of a Successive Approximation Converter

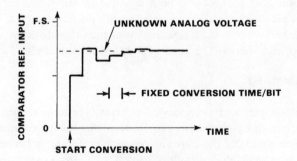

b. Sequential Conversion Process

Figure 4.15. Successive Approximation Conversion

The successive approximation converter is widely used in high performance applications. The conversion time, which is a function of both the electronics and the number of bits, typically ranges about 100 nanoseconds/bit. The converter's accuracy is a function of both the reference source and the comparator.

4.6.4 Dual-Ramp Converter

The dual-ramp converter is also widely used in analog-to-digital processes and is frequently used in digital panel meters and data loggers. However, unlike the successive approximation converter, which converts an unknown analog voltage to a digital value by direct comparison, the dual-ramp converter uses an indirect method. That is, the unknown voltage is first converted to time, and then time is converted to a digital number.

Consider Figure 4.16a, which shows the functional arrangement of the dual-ramp converter. At the start of conversion, the unknown input voltage is applied to an integrator. After a fixed time T_1, as shown in Figure 4.16b, the integrator's input is disconnected from the unknown voltage and connected to a precision reference voltage of opposite polarity. At this time, the integrating capacitor is charged to a value that is proportional to the average value of the input during the integration time. The counter is reset and the reference voltage is then integrated. At some time T_2, the integrator output reaches zero and the counter is stopped. By measuring the time T_1 to T_2, the average value of the input can be established using the following expression:

$$E_{IN} = \frac{T_2 - T_1}{T_1} \times \text{Reference Voltage} \tag{4.7}$$

The dual-ramp converter is highly accurate in that the output does correspond to the average value of the input over the integration time. If the integration time is chosen to be a multiple of line frequency, the converter provides excellent rejection to line frequency noise. Because of the integration time, the technique is substantially slower than the successive approximation converter and, therefore, limited to slow speed applications.

4.7 SUMMARY

In this chapter we have reviewed several of the basic elements of a sampled data system. Our purposes were to illustrate that there are numerous elemental error sources and that there are differences in performance between systems that use low level and high level multiplexing. We have purposely avoided discussing filters at this point, preferring to delay this until we have discussed sampling. In the next chapter, we elaborate on the nature of component errors and establish a method of quantifying measurement accuracy performance.

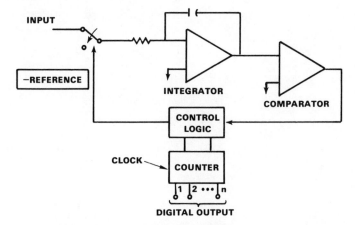

a. Functional Components of a Dual-Ramp Converter

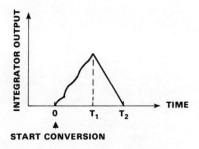

b. Integration Conversion Process

Figure 4.16. Dual-Ramp Conversion

Chapter 5
Error Models and Budgets

5.1 INTRODUCTION

Assume that you are given the task of designing a system for steady-state measurements that will be used to gather data from experiments. These experimental data will be used to produce information that may directly influence critical management decisions. Given this task, what actions can you take to ensure that the quality of the measured results are acceptable? There are two different approaches to this.

First, you may elect to buy the best sensors and data system equipment available and hope that the system's total performance after installation will be acceptable. If this approach is taken, an experiment must be conducted once the total system is installed to ascertain its overall measurement characteristics. Quantifying the measurement system's characteristics is essential if decisions are to be made based on results obtained with this system.

Second, you may elect to use engineering analysis techniques to guide you in designing a system and selecting equipment based on general requirements. Ideally, this analytical approach will provide assurance that the system's composite performance will be acceptable before it is built.

Of these two approaches, obviously the second is preferable. Since the first approach involves a minimum of engineering, there is a risk that the composite system performance as established by experimentation will not be acceptable. Worse yet, this will not be detected and decisions will be made based on assumed performance. While perhaps preferable, the second approach is not a panacea. Systematic design techniques are oftentimes unclear; there is a lack of standards in error classification; and wide variations exist in the way that equipment manufacturer's report performance specifications.

Previously, we established that measurement error is a fundamental design criterion. We saw that since measurements are made to produce information (e.g., consider the parameter BSFC in Example 3.1, which is a function of several measurements), it is essential that the designer begin the process with first establishing the information relationships and the associated goodness requirements of each. Having done so, these can then be used to establish allowable uncertainties in each of the measurements using error propagation techniques. This technique enables us to establish individual measurement accuracy requirements based on actual global performance requirements. Our task for each measurement is to allocate this individual total measurement error to the various measurement chain components (sensor, signal conditioner, amplifier, etc.) such that when these elemental errors are combined, the total measurement error will not exceed the required total measurement error.

5.2 Error Types and Classifications

The total individual measurement error consists of both fixed and random components that combine according to the following relationship:

$$U = \pm (B_T + t_\alpha S_T) \tag{5.1}$$

where

$$B_T = (B_1^2 + B_2^2 + \ldots + B_n^2)^{\frac{1}{2}} \tag{5.2}$$

$$S_T = (S_1^2 + S_2^2 + \ldots + S_n^2)^{\frac{1}{2}} \tag{5.3}$$

B_i and S_i are elemental errors associated with the measurement chain equipment, and t_α is the Student T multiplier chosen based on equivalent degrees of freedom and desired confidence level. Since there are no standards available, the designer is free to select some alternative method of combining errors. Here, the RSS technique has been chosen based on the assumption that, because of the probabilistic nature of errors, there will be some cancellation.

Assuming that the equipment elements of a measurement chain have been selected, then the manufacturer's specifications for each element can be used to identify and quantify the elemental errors. Unfortunately, the lack of standards hampers the designer in both interpreting manufacturer's specifications and in classifying performance specifications as to fixed or random errors. Accordingly, specifications must be interpreted judiciously. Extreme caution should be used with precision errors. The assumption is that these are all one sigma.

When we examine the elements of a measurement chain, we determine that these can be arranged functionally as follows:

- Sensor
- Signal Conditioner
- Amplifier and Filter
- Multiplexer and Converter
- Data Reduction and Analysis

Each of these has elemental errors, which are discussed in the following subsections.

5.2.1 Sensor Errors

Functionally, sensors are used to convert a physical phenomena into a measurable electrical quantity. For passive sensors, critical specifications generally include such performance characteristics as accuracy, linearity, hysteresis, repeatability, and thermal stability.

5.2.1.1 Accuracy

There is an inaccuracy associated with converting a physical phenomena into a measurable electrical quantity. Generally, this is reported by sensor manufacturers as a percent of the full scale sensor rating. Since this is a fixed error and is quantifiable, it is classified as a bias error.

5.2.1.2 Linearity

Linearity is a measure of the deviation of the input-to-output relationship from an ideal linear relationship and is established by analyzing the device's input-to-output relationship. As shown in Figure 5.1, linearity is interpreted as being the observed deviation between the actual input-to-output response and a linear response as defined by the terminal points. While this nonlinearity error varies in magnitude over the range, it is constant at any point. Since this is a fixed error and thus classified as bias, it can be quantified and compensated for. Compensation may be achieved by describing the input-to-output relationship with a higher-order polynomial or equivalent.

5.2.1.3 Hysteresis

Hysteresis is observed to be the phenomenon where the device's output at a given input varies based upon the direction of approach (Figure 5.2) and the magnitude of change. Generally, hysteresis is classified as a random error with no attempt made to compensate or minimize the effects.

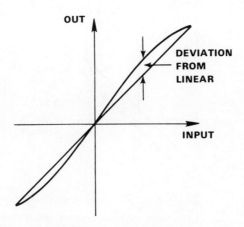

Figure 5.1. Linearity Error

5.2.1.4 Repeatability

Repeatability is observed to be variation in output when the same input is repeatably applied. This is considered to be a random error.

5.2.1.5 Thermal Stability

Whenever a device is subjected to a change in temperature, both its offset and sensitivity may vary. Both errors are considered to be random errors.

5.2.2 Signal Conditioning Errors

The signal conditioning used depends upon the sensor requirements. Here, we are only considering passive sensors that require excitation and suppression. The principal errors attributable to power supply variations include ripple, stability, and regulation. Each of these is considered to be a random error. If used, suppression may be achieved by either voltage insertion or resistive balance. If the voltage insertion technique is used, then the ripple, stability, and regulation parameters of the voltage suppression power supply are of significant concern. If the resistive balance technique is used, the nonlinearity error introduced by the shunting resistors (balance potentiometer in conjunction with the series resistor) must be considered.

5.2.3 Amplifier Errors

Since the amplifier is generally the first active device in the signal path, it is used to discriminate against common-mode voltage, accommodate differences that may exist in zero potential, provide amplification for low level signals, and

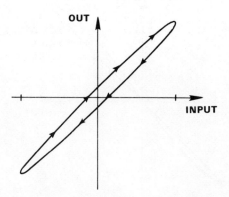

Figure 5.2. Hysteresis Error

limit the signal bandwidth through low pass filtering. Errors associated with each of these functions are described in the following subsection.

5.2.3.1 Common-Mode Voltage

A measure of the ability of a differential amplifier to discriminate against voltages common to both input leads is often presented in manufacturer's specifications as Common-Mode Rejection Ratio (CMRR). This is normally defined for amplifiers as the ratio of the signal gain to the ratio of normal mode signal appearing at the output (that is, between the two output terminals) to the input common-mode voltage. This can be represented as:

$$CMRR = Gain/(\bar{e}_{CMV}/e_{CMV}) \tag{5.4}$$

where $\bar{e}_{CMV}$ is the normal-mode voltage appearing at the output as a result of the input common-mode voltage e_{CMV}. This is often expressed in terms of dB using the following relationship:

$$CMR, dB = 20 \log (CMRR) \tag{5.5}$$

Thus, if we can measure or estimate the CMV, then we can quantify the error using the following relationship:

$$\bar{e}_{CMV} = (G)(e_{CMV}) \left| \log^{-1} \left(\frac{CMR, dB}{20} \right) \right. \tag{5.6}$$

Since errors attributable to common-mode voltage are often mistakenly related to only differences in ground potential, they are often ignored. For strain gage applications with a grounded power supply, there is a common mode voltage of approximately one-half the excitation. This type of constant offset is classified as a bias error and can be compensated for.

5.2.3.2 Normal Mode

Differences in zero potential can generate normal mode voltages if the signal lines are not balanced (see Figure 4.8). This error is presented as a difference in voltage between the amplifier's input terminals and thus cannot be distinguished from an actual input signal. Because of the variability of this error, it is classified as a random error.

5.2.3.3 Amplification

Static performance specifications for amplifiers typically include linearity, gain accuracy, and temperature coefficient. As discussed in Section 5.2.1.2, linearity is considered to be a bias error. Gain accuracy (Figure 5.3) is defined as a deviation from nominal gain. As shown, this error is constant at a specific input voltage. Accordingly, gain accuracy is classified as a bias error.

Gain accuracy, offset, and linearity of a device are all affected by variations in ambient temperature. Specifications are generally stated in terms of parts per million (ppm) of full scale per degree Celsius. Thus, if a device that has a gain temperature coefficient (tempco) of ± 20 ppm/$^\circ$C is subjected to temperature variations of $\pm 5^\circ$C about a mean temperature, then the resulting gain change expressed in percent of full scale is:

$$
\begin{aligned}
\text{Gain Change, \%} &= (\text{Tempco})(\text{Temp Change})(100) \qquad (5.7)\\
&= (\pm 20 \text{ ppm/}^\circ\text{C})(5^\circ\text{C})(100)\\
&= \pm 0.01\%
\end{aligned}
$$

Because of the variability of errors attributable to ambient temperature changes, they are classified as random errors. Note that when the effects are calculated as above, we are stating that this is the maximum change we anticipate.

5.2.3.4 Filtering

The primary purpose of the filter is to limit the bandwidth to reduce errors associated with sampling. As such, the filter introduces both static and dynamic errors. Static errors are generally restricted to gain related errors such as gain accuracy, linearity, and thermal induced errors such as offset and gain.

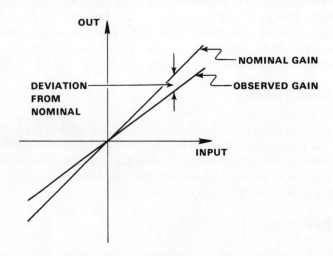

Figure 5.3. Gain Accuracy Error

5.2.4 Multiplexing and Conversion

Static errors associated with multiplexing are generally restricted to adjacent channel interference (crosstalk) and transfer accuracy (i.e., gain related errors). Crosstalk is classified as a random error.

Static errors associated with analog-to-digital conversion may include typical gain-related errors if the converter includes either a programmable gain amplifier (PGA) or a sample-and-hold, as well as the quantization error attributable to conversion. Quantization is classified as a random error equal to $\pm \frac{1}{2}$ LSB, where LSB is the value of the least significant bit. By definition, the extremes for this random error is $\pm \frac{1}{2}$ LSB.

5.2.5 Data Reduction and Analysis

Often overlooked error sources are data reduction and analysis. While there is a concern for error attributable to round-off and truncation — especially for parameters requiring double precision computation — the most significant errors are the large unknown biases. These errors are those caused by poor programming practices and the lack of attention to implementation details by the systems engineer. Thus, for example, a decision may be made, by implementers who are unaware of the consequences, to use a single sample to characterize a measurement that has an amplitude variation with time or to use nonstandard interpolating polynomials for thermocouples.

5.3 ERROR MODELS

A graphical aid in establishing system error, where a system is an integration of different manufacturers's equipment, can be realized using an error model. Essentially, an error model is a block diagram of the different system components, including sensor, required to implement a measurement. Once the component arrangement is established and the equipment selected, the composite performance can be established by analyzing the different manufacturers's specifications. Since some manufacturers's specifications are in terms of static level, it is important that the gains be chosen and all errors computed at this level.

Errors for each system component are first identified and then classified as either bias or precision. These elemental errors are then combined using the RSS technique to produce component bias and precision errors. The various bias and precision errors for the different system components are then further pooled to establish total system bias and precision and, thus, measurement uncertainty.

Depending upon the measurement to be made, different types of equipment may be required for a multichannel system. Thus, a designer may need to develop several error models that are representative of the measurements to be made. To illustrate the technique, error models for measuring miscellaneous analog voltages, temperature with both thermocouples and RTD's, and other phenomena with strain gage sensors are presented in the following subsections.

5.3.1 Analog Voltage

The analog voltage static error model (Figure 5.4) is the simplest since less equipment is required. For completeness, each component shown, with the exceptions of the sensor and ADC, is assumed to have a gain stage and, thus, will exhibit gain-related errors. Additionally, each component will exhibit errors attributable to ambient temperature changes and noise. Although the filter and sample-and-hold (S/H) affect dynamic performance more than static performance, they have been included for completeness.

As shown, any errors that may be attributable to common-mode voltage (CMV) are included as part of the differential amplifier's errors. These include the bias error ($\bar{e}_{CMV}$) attributable to the inherent CMR characteristics of the differential amplifier and the normal mode precision error attributable to CMV in conjunction with signal line imbalance. If $\bar{e}_{CMV}$ is not constant, this error should be classified as a random rather than a bias error. By including only these CMV-related errors with the differential amplifier, it is assumed that there is no CMV with the other system components.

To quantify the errors, it is first necessary to perform the following:

1. **Establish signal levels.** To accomplish this, the sensor's output range as well as the point to be analyzed are first established. Using this, gains for both the differential amplifier and the PGA are chosen in concert to accommodate the entire sensor range based on maximizing the ADC's resolution.

2. **Quantify the maximum ambient temperature change for each component.** This is used in conjunction with each component's thermal related performance specifications to establish the absolute maximum variation that is expected.

3. **Quantify CMV.** This is used in conjunction with the amplifier's CMRR to establish the fixed offset error.

4. **Quantify Line Imbalance.** This is used in conjunction with CMV to determine the normal mode error.

Following these actions, the manufacturer's specifications for each system component are analyzed to establish the various elemental errors. Depending upon the equipment chosen, various error specifications may be lumped together or, worse yet, not reported. Regardless, engineering judgment is required in interpreting a manufacturer's literature.

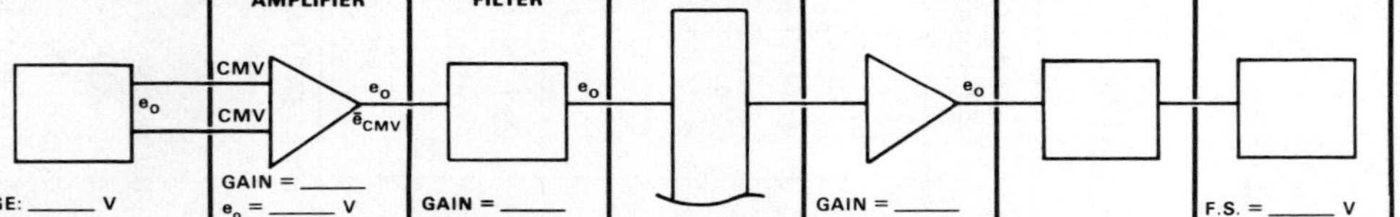

SENSOR	DIFFERENTIAL AMPLIFIER	ACTIVE FILTER	MPLXR	PGA	S/H	ADC
RANGE: ______ V e_o = ______ V	GAIN = ______ e_o = ______ V CMV ______ V	GAIN = ______ e_o = ______ V		GAIN = ______ e_o = ______ V		F.S. = ______ V NO. BITS = ______
MFG. ______ MODEL ______	MFG. ______ MODEL ______	MFG. ______ MODEL ______	MFG. ______ MODEL ______	MFG. ______ MODEL ______	MFG. ______ MODEL ______	MFG. ______ MODEL ______
	GAIN ACCURACY b6.1 = ______	GAIN ACCURACY b5.1 = ______	GAIN ACCURACY b4.1 = ______	GAIN ACCURACY b3.1 = ______	GAIN ACCURACY b2.1 = ______	GAIN ACCURACY b1.1 = ______
	LINEARITY b6.2 = ______	LINEARITY b5.2 = ______	LINEARITY b4.2 = ______	LINEARITY b3.2 = ______	LINEARITY b2.2 = ______	LINEARITY b1.2 = ______
	OFFSET b6.3 = ______	OFFSET b5.3 = ______	OFFSET b4.3 = ______	OFFSET b3.3 = ______	OFFSET b2.3 = ______	OFFSET b1.3 = ______
	$\bar{e}_{CMV}$ b6.4 = ______					
	NOISE S6.1 = ______	NOISE S5.1 = ______	NOISE S4.1 = ______	NOISE S3.1 = ______	NOISE S2.1 = ______	NOISE S1.1 = ______
	GAIN STABILITY S6.2 = ______	GAIN STABILITY S5.2 = ______	GAIN STABILITY S4.2 = ______	GAIN STABILITY S3.2 = ______	GAIN STABILITY S2.2 = ______	GAIN STABILITY S1.2 = ______
	ZERO STABILITY S6.3 = ______	ZERO STABILITY S5.3 = ______	ZERO STABILITY S4.3 = ______	ZERO STABILITY S3.3 = ______	ZERO STABILITY S2.3 = ______	ZERO STABILITY S1.3 = ______
	NORMAL MODE S6.4 = ______		CROSSTALK S4.4 = ______			QUANTIZATION S1.4 = ______
B7 = S7 =	B6 = S6 =	B5 = S5 =	B4 = S4 =	B3 = S3 =	B2 = S2 =	B1 = S1 =

Figure 5.4. Static Error Model for Analog Voltage Measurements

5.3.2 Error Model for Temperature Measurements Using Thermocouples

Thermocouples are differential measurement devices; that is, the emf generated is a function of the difference in temperature between the unknown sensed temperature and a reference junction. There are several areas of concern regarding accuracy.

First, there will be a difference in the emf vs. temperature characteristics between manufactured thermocouple wire and the standards published by the National Bureau of Standards. This is a consequence of both the purity and homogeneity of the material used. Table 5.1 lists these errors for several of the standard thermocouples. These are interpreted as bias errors.

Table 5.1. Typical Published Errors for Thermocouples

THERMOCOUPLE MATERIALS	ISA TYPE	TEMP RANGE	STANDARD ERRORS	SPECIAL ERRORS
COPPER/CONSTANTAN	T	−300°F TO −150°F	—	±1% Rdg
		−150°F TO −75°F	±2% Rdg	±1% Rdg
		−75°F TO 200°F	±1.5°F	±0.75% Rdg
		200°F TO 700°F	±0.75% Rdg	±0.36% Rdg
IRON/CONSTANTAN	J	32°F TO 530°F	±4°F	±2°F
		530°F TO 1400°F	±0.75% Rdg	±0.36% Rdg
CHROMEL/CONSTANTAN	E	32°F TO 600°F	±3°F	±2°F
		600°F TO 1600°F	±0.5% Rdg	±0.36 Rdg
CHROMEL/ALUMEL	K	32°F TO 530°F	±4°F	±2°F
		530°F TO 2300°F	±0.75% Rdg	±0.36% Rdg
PLATINUM - 30% RHODIUM/PLATINUM	B	1600°F TO 3100°F	±0.5% Rdg	—

Second, there are errors associated with measuring the analog voltage, which for a given thermocouple can be stated in degrees. As shown in Figure 5.5, the generated signals are low level (i.e., less than 100 mV). Because the ADC's full scale input range is typically ±5 V or ±10 V, the low level thermocouple signals must be amplified to maximize the measurement's resolution. Gains should be selected based on thermocouple range and ADC full scale input and should be used to compute the errors associated with measuring this voltage.

Third, there is an error associated with the reference junction. Because thermocouples are differential devices, a reference junction is required. Temperature reference junctions can either be ambient temperature junctions or constant temperature junctions. If an ambient junction is used, the temperature must be precisely measured. This is normally accomplished using an RTD.

Accordingly, there are errors associated with measuring the junction's temperature using an RTD. If, instead of an ambient junction, a constant temperature junction is used, there are errors associated with maintaining this temperature constant. That is, there will be some temperature cycling as a result of the regulatory action of the junction controller. Regardless of the type of junction used, the total measurement error is the RSS of the analog voltage measurement error and the error associated with either measuring the junction temperature or with maintaining that temperature constant.

Finally, there is an error associated with converting the measured analog voltage into a temperature. Traditionally, characteristic emf vs. temperature tables, which have been published by the National Bureau of Standards, are used to convert measured emf to temperature. Because the tables are cumbersome to implement and require interpolation, polynomials for several types have been developed and are used. These typically introduce errors less than $\pm 0.2°$C.

Figure 5.6 illustrates an error model that can be used to quantify the total measurement error in temperature when thermocouples are used.

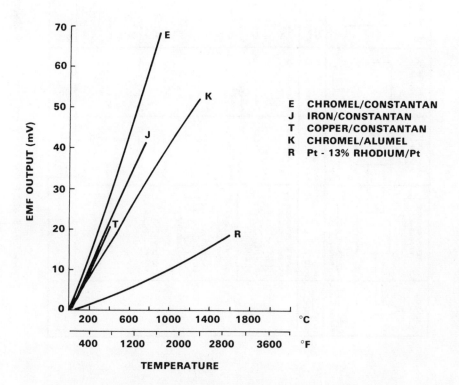

Figure 5.5. Thermocouple EMF vs. Temperature Curves (0°C Ref.)

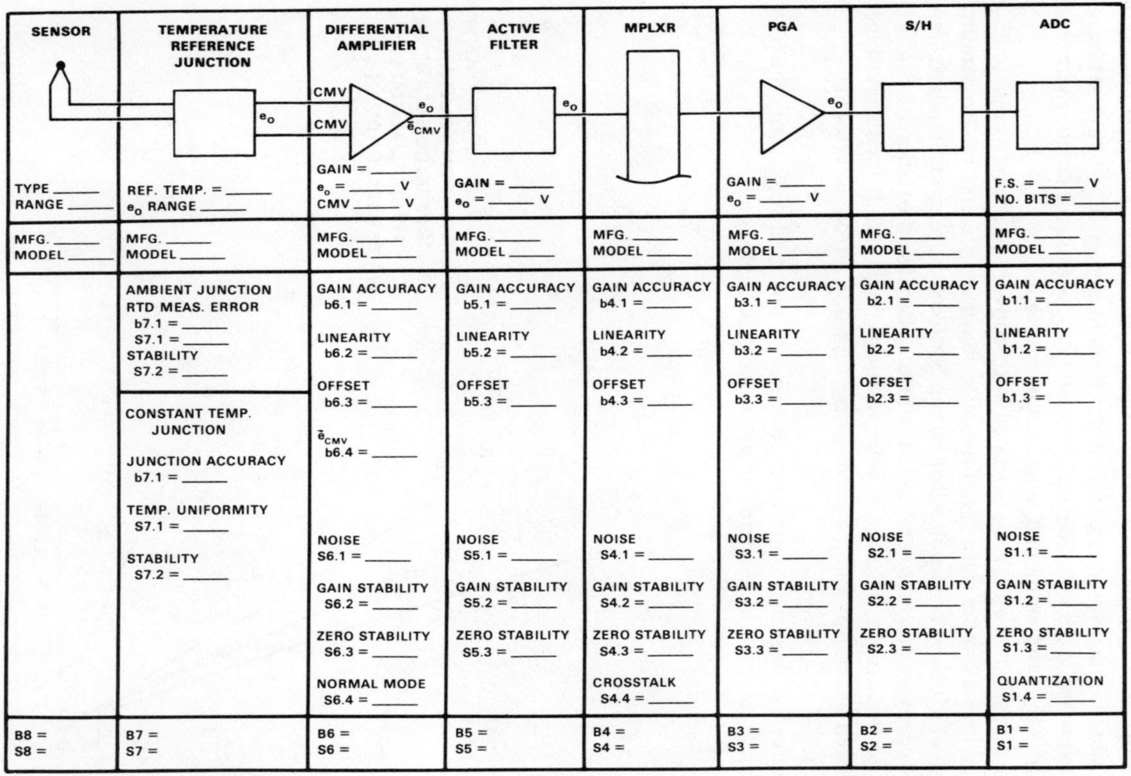

SENSOR	TEMPERATURE REFERENCE JUNCTION	DIFFERENTIAL AMPLIFIER	ACTIVE FILTER	MPLXR	PGA	S/H	ADC
TYPE ___ RANGE ___	REF. TEMP. = ___ e_o RANGE ___	CMV ___ V e_o = ___ V GAIN = ___ CMV = ___ V	GAIN = ___ e_o = ___ V		GAIN = ___ e_o = ___ V		F.S. = ___ V NO. BITS = ___
MFG. ___ MODEL ___	MFG. ___ MODEL ___	MFG. ___ MODEL ___	MFG. ___ MODEL ___	MFG. ___ MODEL ___	MFG. ___ MODEL ___	MFG. ___ MODEL ___	MFG. ___ MODEL ___
	AMBIENT JUNCTION RTD MEAS. ERROR b7.1 = ___ STABILITY S7.1 = ___ S7.2 = ___ CONSTANT TEMP. JUNCTION JUNCTION ACCURACY b7.1 = ___ TEMP. UNIFORMITY S7.1 = ___ STABILITY S7.2 = ___	GAIN ACCURACY b6.1 = ___ LINEARITY b6.2 = ___ OFFSET b6.3 = ___ $\bar{e}_{CMV}$ b6.4 = ___	GAIN ACCURACY b5.1 = ___ LINEARITY b5.2 = ___ OFFSET b5.3 = ___	GAIN ACCURACY b4.1 = ___ LINEARITY b4.2 = ___ OFFSET b4.3 = ___	GAIN ACCURACY b3.1 = ___ LINEARITY b3.2 = ___ OFFSET b3.3 = ___	GAIN ACCURACY b2.1 = ___ LINEARITY b2.2 = ___ OFFSET b2.3 = ___	GAIN ACCURACY b1.1 = ___ LINEARITY b1.2 = ___ OFFSET b1.3 = ___
		NOISE S6.1 = ___ GAIN STABILITY S6.2 = ___ ZERO STABILITY S6.3 = ___ NORMAL MODE S6.4 = ___	NOISE S5.1 = ___ GAIN STABILITY S5.2 = ___ ZERO STABILITY S5.3 = ___	NOISE S4.1 = ___ GAIN STABILITY S4.2 = ___ ZERO STABILITY S4.3 = ___ CROSSTALK S4.4 = ___	NOISE S3.1 = ___ GAIN STABILITY S3.2 = ___ ZERO STABILITY S3.3 = ___	NOISE S2.1 = ___ GAIN STABILITY S2.2 = ___ ZERO STABILITY S2.3 = ___	NOISE S1.1 = ___ GAIN STABILITY S1.2 = ___ ZERO STABILITY S1.3 = ___ QUANTIZATION S1.4 = ___
B8 = S8 =	B7 = S7 =	B6 = S6 =	B5 = S5 =	B4 = S4 =	B3 = S3 =	B2 = S2 =	B1 = S1 =

Figure 5.6. Static Error Model for Temperature Measurements Using Thermocouples

5.3.3 Error Model for Temperature Measurement Using RTD's

Resistance Temperature Devices (RTD) are frequently used for applications requiring more accurate temperature measurements than can be realized using thermocouples. RTD's work on the principle that temperature affects the electrical resistance of a metal. If, for a given material, the resistance vs. temperature characteristics can be established and if a means of measuring these resistance changes can be developed, then temperature can be measured.

Although RTD's are considered variable resistors and thus require but two wires, they are often supplied in two-, three-, and four-wire configurations (Figure 5.7). As shown, both of the two- and three-wire RTD configurations are normally arranged as Wheatstone bridges with a constant voltage excitation. The four-wire configuration is not generally used in a bridge arrangement. Instead, a constant current is used to excite the sensor.

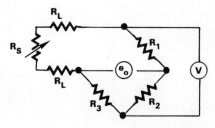

a. Two-Wire configuration

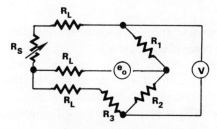

b. Three-Wire Configuration

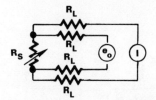

c. Four-Wire Configuration

Figure 5.7. Common RTD Circuit Configurations

The errors associated with RTD's include those with conditioning the sensor and with measuring the analog voltage. Both identifying and quantifying errors associated with the two- and three-wire configurations can be established by analyzing the sensor output voltage relationship. For the three-wire configuration, the following relationship is used:

$$e_o = V \left[\frac{R_3 + R_L}{R_s + 2R_L + R_3} - \frac{R_2}{R_1 + R_2} \right] \tag{5.8}$$

where R_1, R_2, and R_3 are bridge completion resistors, R_L is line resistance, V is excitation voltage, and R_s is the sensor's resistance. Using a Taylor series we can establish the following:

$$\Delta e_o = \frac{\partial e_o}{\partial R_s} \Delta R_s + \frac{\partial e_o}{\partial R_L} \Delta R_L + \frac{\partial e_o}{\partial V} \Delta V + \frac{\partial e_o}{\partial R_1} \Delta R_1 + \frac{\partial e_o}{\partial R_2} \Delta R_2 + \frac{\partial e_o}{\partial R_3} \Delta R_3 + R \tag{5.9}$$

Of interest is how the output (e_o) changes as a result of changes in the RTD sensor. Thus,

$$\Delta e_o = \frac{-(R_3 + R_L) V}{(R_s + 2R_L + R_3)^2} \Delta R_s \tag{5.10}$$

Thus, the relationship is nonlinear. This nonlinearity effect can be minimized by making the bridge completion resistor R_3 much greater than R_s (this is also desirable to reduce the current flow through the sensor and thus minimize self-heating effects). Typically, if R_3 is chosen to be 100 times as large as R_s, the nonlinearity error is approximately 0.1 percent.

To evaluate the effects of power supply fluctuations, we can use the following:

$$\Delta e_o = \frac{\partial e_o}{\partial V} \Delta V \tag{5.11}$$

where

$$\frac{\partial e_o}{\partial V} = \left[\frac{R_3 + R_L}{R_s + 2R_L + R_3} - \frac{R_2}{R_1 + R_2} \right] \tag{5.12}$$

Based on this, we have a method for quantifying the effects of power supply variations.

Figure 5.8 illustrates the error model for temperature measurements using RTD's. The only signal conditioning errors shown are those attributable to power supply variations (classified as random errors) and the nonlinearity error attributable to bridge completion resistor R_3 (classified as a bias error). Equations 5.8 and 5.9 can be used to quantify these errors as well as to investigate the effects of line resistance (classified as bias) and variations in the bridge completion resistors resulting from temperature change (classified as random errors).

Example 5.1

Problem Statement

Using a 100-ohm RTD configured in a three-wire mode with bridge completion resistors as shown in the sketch below, determine the effects that a line resistance, R_L, of 1.6 ohms (1.6 ohms is the equivalent resistance for 100 feet of AWG22 wire) would have on the measured voltage, e_o, if a constant voltage excitation is used.

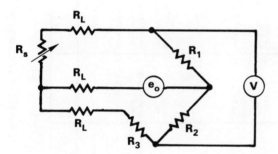

$$R_1 = 100 \ \Omega$$
$$R_2 = 9{,}900 \ \Omega$$
$$R_3 = 9{,}900 \ \Omega$$
$$R_L = 1.6 \ \Omega$$
$$R_s = 80 \ \Omega$$
$$V = 10 \ V$$

Solution

We can perform a simple circuit analysis to determine the output voltage e_o with $R_L = o$ and again with $R_L = 1.6 \ \Omega$. This difference can then be used to establish the percent difference in e_o, which is attributable to line resistance R_L.

For $R_L = 0$, $e_o = 0.0198396 \ V$
For $R_L = 1.6 \ \Omega$, $e_o = 0.0178653 \ V$

Thus, the error expressed as a percent of reading is:

$$\text{Error, } \% = \frac{0.00197}{0.01984} \times 100 = 9.9\%$$

	RTD	SIGNAL CONDITIONER	DIFFERENTIAL AMPLIFIER	ACTIVE FILTER	MPLXR	PGA	S/H	ADC
	R_{NOM} = ____ ΔR = ____	EXCITATION = ____ e_o RANGE = ____ e_o = ____	GAIN = ____ e_o = ____ V CMV = ____ V	GAIN = ____ e_o = ____ V		GAIN = ____ e_o = ____ V		F.S. = ____ V NO. BITS = ____
	MFG. ____ MODEL ____	MFG. ____ MODEL ____	MFG. ____ MODEL ____	MFG. ____ MODEL ____	MFG. ____ MODEL ____	MFG. ____ MODEL ____	MFG. ____ MODEL ____	MFG. ____ MODEL ____
		2-W OR 3-W CONFIG NONLINEARITY b7.1 = ____ LINE RESISTANCE b7.2 = ____ LOAD REGULATION S7.1 = ____ LINE REGULATION S7.2 = ____ SUPPLY RIPPLE S7.3 = ____	GAIN ACCURACY b6.1 = ____ LINEARITY b6.2 = ____ OFFSET b6.3 = ____	GAIN ACCURACY b5.1 = ____ LINEARITY b5.2 = ____ OFFSET b5.3 = ____	GAIN ACCURACY b4.1 = ____ LINEARITY b4.2 = ____ OFFSET b4.3 = ____	GAIN ACCURACY b3.1 = ____ LINEARITY b3.2 = ____ OFFSET b3.3 = ____	GAIN ACCURACY b2.1 = ____ LINEARITY b2.2 = ____ OFFSET b2.3 = ____	GAIN ACCURACY b1.1 = ____ LINEARITY b1.2 = ____ OFFSET b1.3 = ____
		4-W CONFIG LOAD REGULATION S7.1 = ____ LINE REGULATION S7.2 = ____ SUPPLY RIPPLE S7.3 = ____	$\bar{e}_{CMV}$ b6.4 = ____					
			NOISE S6.1 = ____ GAIN STABILITY S6.2 = ____ ZERO STABILITY S6.3 = ____ NORMAL MODE S6.4 = ____	NOISE S5.1 = ____ GAIN STABILITY S5.2 = ____ ZERO STABILITY S5.3 = ____	NOISE S4.1 = ____ GAIN STABILITY S4.2 = ____ ZERO STABILITY S4.3 = ____ CROSSTALK S4.4 = ____	NOISE S3.1 = ____ GAIN STABILITY S3.2 = ____ ZERO STABILITY S3.3 = ____	NOISE S2.1 = ____ GAIN STABILITY S2.2 = ____ ZERO STABILITY S2.3 = ____	NOISE S1.1 = ____ GAIN STABILITY S1.2 = ____ ZERO STABILITY S1.3 = ____ QUANTIZATION S1.4 = ____
	B8 = ____ S8 = ____	B7 = ____ S7 = ____	B6 = ____ S6 = ____	B5 = ____ S5 = ____	B4 = ____ S4 = ____	B3 = ____ S3 = ____	B2 = ____ S2 = ____	B1 = ____ S1 = ____

Figure 5.8. Static Error Model For Temperature Measurements Using RTD's

An alternate method is to use the partial derivative. Thus

$$\frac{\partial e_o}{\partial R_L} = \frac{(R_s - R_3)\,V}{(R_s + 2R_L + R_3)^2} = -986 \times 10^{-6}$$

The error corresponding to a line resistance of 1.6 ohms is:

$$\Delta e_o = \frac{\partial e_o}{\partial R_L}\,\Delta R_L$$

$$\Delta e_o = (-986 \times 10^{-6})\,(1.6)$$

$$\Delta e_o = 0.00197\text{ V}$$

which is what we determined above.

NOTE: The error attributable to line resistance is a bias error that can be calibrated out, assuming that the line resistance remains constant.

Example 5.2

Problem Statement

Assume that the lead resistance for Example 5.1 is exposed to a temperature change of $50°\text{C}$ and that the wire has a temperature coefficient of $4330\text{ ppm}/°\text{C}$. Determine the error introduced in the measured voltage e_o.

Solution

The change in e_o attributable to a change in R_L is:

$$\Delta e_o = \frac{\partial e_o}{\partial R_L}\,\Delta R_L$$

where

$$\frac{\partial e_o}{\partial R_L} = \frac{(R_2 - R_3)\,V}{(R_s + 2R_L + R_3)^2}$$

and

$$\Delta R_L = (4330\text{ ppm}/°\text{C})\,(50°\text{C})\,(1.6\ \Omega/10^6)$$

Using values for R_2, R_3, and R_s from Example 5.1, we find:

$$\frac{\partial e_o}{\partial R_L} = (-986 \times 10^{-6})$$

$$\Delta R_L = 0.3464 \ \Omega$$

Thus

$$\Delta e_o = -341.6 \times 10^{-6} \ \text{V}$$

Expressed as a percentage error using $e_o = 0.01984$ from Example 5.1 gives:

$$\text{Error, \%} = \frac{-341.6 \times 10^{-6}}{0.01984} \quad -1.7\%$$

Example 5.3

Problem Statement

Using a 100-ohm RTD configured in a three-wire mode with a constant current excitation applied as shown in the sketch below, determine the effects that a line resistance of 1.6 ohms would have on the measured voltage.

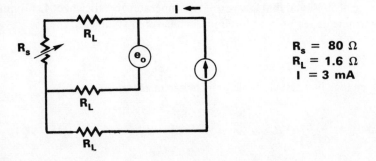

$$R_s = 80 \ \Omega$$
$$R_L = 1.6 \ \Omega$$
$$I = 3 \ \text{mA}$$

Solution

The effect of R_L on e_o can be determined as follows:

$$\Delta e_o = \frac{\partial e_o}{\partial R_L} \ \Delta R_L$$

where

$$e_o = I(R_s + R_L)$$

and

$$\frac{\partial e_o}{\partial R_L} = IR_s$$

Thus,

$$\Delta e_o = (0.24) + I\Delta R_L$$

For $\Delta R_L = 1.6$,

$$\Delta e_o = 0.2448$$

The error, expressed in percent of e_o, is:

$$\text{Error, \%} = \frac{0.0048}{0.24} = 2\%$$

Note that this is a fixed error and can be eliminated by calibration.

Example 5.4

Problem Statement

Determine the effect that line resistance, R_L, has on an 100-ohm RTD configuration in a four-wire mode with a constant current excitation applied as shown in the sketch below.

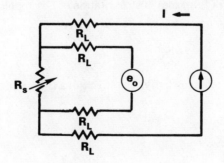

Solution

The output, e_o, can be described by the following equation

$$e_o = R_s I$$

As shown, R_L has no effect on e_o.

5.3.4 Error Model for Strain Gage Measurements

Various phenomena such as pressure and force utilize strain gage techniques to convert the unknown phenomena into measurable electrical quantities. Strain gages are passive sensors and thus require excitation. Additionally, the bridge may have a constant offset at zero measurement as a consequence of component degradation. To maximize system resolution, it is desirable to suppress this offset. This may be accomplished by either inserting a voltage of equal and opposite polarity in series with the signal lead or by applying unequal shunts to the active bridge arms (see Figure 4.4).

Principal errors associated with strain gage sensors include those associated with the signal conditioning, measuring the analog output voltage, and an inherent CMV error (assuming a grounded excitation supply is used). Signal conditioning errors include excitation power supply variations (classified as random errors) and offset suppression-related errors. If the voltage suppression technique is used, then critical errors are variations in the suppression power supply. These are generally classified as random errors. If, instead of voltage suppression, the resistive balance technique is used, the principal error resulting from shunting active bridge arms is nonlinearity (classified as bias). An inherent CMV error is the result of having a CMV of approximately onehalf the bridge excitation present at all times. This is classified as a bias error.

Figure 5.9 illustrates a strain gage error model. To evaluate the effects of excitation power supply variations, the following technique is used. Strain gage sensitivity is generally stated in terms of output voltage (e_o) per volt of excitation (e.g., 3 mV/V for full scale). If an excitation of E is applied, then the output is:

$$e_o = CE \tag{5.13}$$

where C is the full scale sensitivity. The effects of a change in excitation voltage (ΔE) is:

$$\Delta e_o = \frac{\partial e_o}{\partial E} \Delta E \tag{5.14}$$

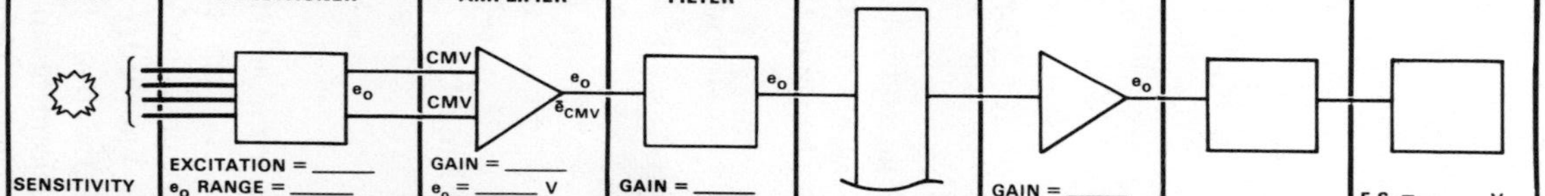

Figure 5.9. Static Error Model For Measurements Using Strain Gages

where

$$\frac{\partial e_o}{\partial E} = C \tag{5.15}$$

Thus,

$$\Delta e_o = C \Delta E \tag{5.16}$$

In terms of percentage, we obtain

$$\frac{\Delta e_o}{e_o} = \frac{C \Delta E}{e_o} \tag{5.17}$$

Substituting for e_o yields

$$\frac{\Delta e_o}{e_o} = \frac{C \Delta E}{CE} = \frac{\Delta E}{E} \tag{5.18}$$

Thus a percentage variation in excitation voltage relates to an equivalent percentage change in bridge sensitivity. Accordingly, if the excitation voltage changes by ± 0.1 percent, this is equivalent to a ± 0.1 percent change in the bridge output.

If resistive balancing is used, the nonlinearity error for a fully active bridge can be approximated as:

$$\text{Error, \%} = \frac{-R}{(4R_{\text{SERIES}})} \times 100 \tag{5.19}$$

where R is the bridge resistance and R_{SERIES} is as defined in Figure 4.4a.

5.4 SUMMARY

The static error models presented in Section 5.3 provide a method for quantifying measurement error based on selected equipment. As such, this enables us to directly compare the performance of different configurations. We can use this understanding of how errors combine along with knowledge of achievable component performance to establish a measurement error budget. If we establish budgets by considering the different types of measurements to be made using a multichannel system, then we can determine specifications for the common analog voltage measurement components. Difficulty in achieving these specifications with common equipment would prompt consideration of multiple systems.

In this chapter, we concerned ourselves with static errors for several typical measurements by analyzing the relationship of the sensor to the data system. We saw that simple analysis techniques can help us to understand the errors — even to uncover potentially large unknown biases such as those caused by R_L for RTD's. We also saw that these analytical techniques can be used as a means of justifying equipment specifications. The errors we discussed here are all static errors. There are others we term **dynamic** that relate to the sampling phenomenon. This is the subject of our next chapter.

Chapter 6
Sampling Fundamentals

6.1 INTRODUCTION

The number of discrete samples used to represent a continuous signal whose amplitude is changing with time is of primary importance in a sampled data system. Since a denumerable set of samples is used to represent a continuum, information is lost in the process that may significantly distort the interpretation. Consequently, the question that must be addressed by the designer is whether or not the sampled data will be sufficient to describe the continuous variable. Failure to provide the proper sampling characteristics can potentially jeopardize the data system's function by introducing errors that are significantly greater than all other system errors. Here, we are concerned with the nature of sampling errors and will seek ways to minimize their magnitude. As we will see, these errors can never be completely eliminated. The designer then is confronted with deciding not how to eliminate these errors but rather how to economically manage their effects.

The errors we are concerned with are directly related to the measurement application. If, for example, our interest in the incoming signals can be restricted to the time domain, the errors of interest to us are only those that affect amplitude. That is, our concern may be with capturing the extremes of an input (i.e., peak or minimum), finding the average value, establishing the root-mean-square, or performing some other simple time analysis. For applications such as this, which involve only time domain analysis, we categorize the errors that are attributable to sampling and that affect amplitude accuracy as Type I Errors.

If our interest is with frequency domain analysis, the errors that concern us are, in all likelihood, the Type I errors associated with amplitude and, in addition, those that affect our analysis of a set of denumerable samples being used to represent a continuum. For example, our interest may be with analyzing a complex input waveform to determine the frequency content and the energy associated with each discrete frequency. Errors introduced by the sampling process that affect frequency are referred to as Type II Errors.

For either error type, there are several key areas of concern. First of all, the quantization process takes a finite time. Since our inputs are dynamic signals (i.e., they are changing with time), we need to be concerned with how much our input can change during this conversion process. Secondly, we need to concern ourselves with the sampling frequency; that is, how often must we sample to ensure that no significant information is lost. In addition to these two major items, we must also be concerned with sampling duration, aggregate throughput, and what we are to do with these sampled data. The first two concerns influence the conversion equipment, whereas the latter concerns influence the processor selection.

6.2 SAMPLING PROCESS

6.2.1 Introduction

Consider Figure 6.1 where a function of time denoted $f_1(t)$ is input to a digital sampler. The sampler acts as a switch, permitting the sampler output to instantaneously equal the function $f_1(t)$ whenever the switch is closed. Mathematically, we can represent the sampler by a transfer function whose numeric value is one the instant the switch is closed and zero at all other times. That is, if we denote the sampler transfer function as $f_2(t)$, then

$$f_2(t) = \sum_{n=-\infty}^{\infty} \delta(t - nT) \tag{6.1}$$

where $\delta(t - nT)$ is a unit impulse occurring at $t = nT$. As illustrated in Figure 6.2, $f_2(t)$ consists of an infinite number of impulses with period T. Using this

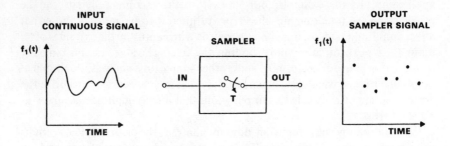

Figure 6.1. Simplified Digital Sampling Process

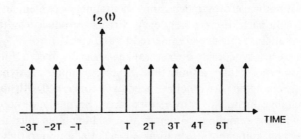

Figure 6.2. Infinite Number of Sampling Function Impulses

analogy to describe digital sampling, the sampler's output in the time domain can be considered to be the product of $f_1(t)$ and $f_2(t)$. That is,

$$\text{Output} = f_1(t) \cdot f_2(t)$$

$$= \sum_{n=-\infty}^{\infty} f_1(t) \, \delta \, (t - nT) \tag{6.2}$$

The output of the sampler is shown graphically in Figure 6.1. Obviously, information has been lost in the sampling process since we are now representing a continuum with a finite number of impulse samples. Is this loss of information significant? To answer this, we need to determine whether or not we can reconstruct the input function $f_1(t)$ from this set of discrete samples.

We can obtain an insight into this reconstruction process by considering Figure 6.3. Here a 3-hertz sinusoidal has been sampled every 0.2 seconds. As a result of this 5-hertz sampling frequency, extraneous signals appear as 2 and 8 hertz sinusoidals. There is, in fact, an infinite number of sinusoidals that can be constructed to pass through the sampled points. Careful study of these extraneous signals, which we term aliases, indicates that the 2-hertz signal represents the difference between the sampling frequency and the input sinusoidal and the 8-hertz signal represents their sum. Intuitively, we suspect that there is a relationship between the sampling and signal frequencies. To establish this relationship, we need to consider the sampling process in the frequency domain.

6.2.2 Spectra

A time domain function, denoted $f(t)$, can be transformed into an equivalent frequency domain function, $F(f)$, using the Fourier transform. The Fourier transform is an integral transformation of the form

$$F(f) = \int_{-\infty}^{\infty} f(T) \, e^{-j2\pi ft} \, dt \tag{6.3}$$

where f is frequency and j is the complex variable equal to $\sqrt{-1}$. There are certain conditions that must be satisfied to assure the existence of $F(f)$. Although they are considered minimal, they should be verified when transforming signals of an unusual character.

Figure 6.4 illustrates some of the more common time domain functions and their transforms. The plots shown of frequency vs. amplitude are referred to as **spectrum plots**. In Figure 6.4a, sinusoidal waveforms are represented in the frequency domain by vertical lines. In Figure 6.4b, the richness of a pulse waveform in harmonics is evident. Figure 6.4c illustrates the transform of the impulse sampling function described previously. Figure 6.4d illustrates the general appearance of a commonly encountered random function. Here, we see that the magnitude diminishes as frequency increases; that is, as frequency increases, the corresponding amplitude decreases.

The function illustrated in Figure 6.4d is representative of the type of measurement system inputs we encounter; that is, the input is a complex waveform consisting of various frequencies at different amplitudes. As shown, the function has a unique representation in the frequency domain characterized by energy being present at various discrete frequencies extending from zero to f_c. Since this continuous function is represented by a finite number of discrete samples in a sampled data system, our immediate concern is with the frequencies corresponding to this sampled function. Based on the data presented in Figure 6.3, we suspect that the sampled function frequency differs from that shown in Figure 6.4d. To gain an insight into this, we need to examine the product of $f_1(t)$ and $f_2(t)$ in the frequency domain.

6.2.3 Convolution

In the time domain, the sampler's output is considered to be the product of the input function $f_1(t)$ and the sampler function $f_2(t)$. If both functions are

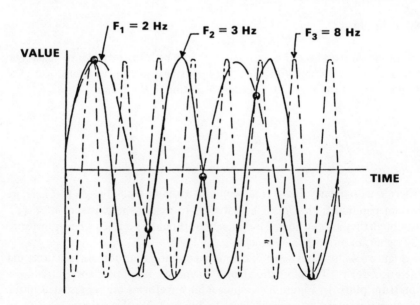

Figure 6.3. Alias Signals Having Same Value at Sampling Times

FUNCTION

SPECTRA

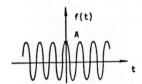

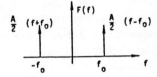

a. Sinusoidal Functions

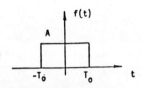

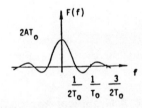

b. Square Wave

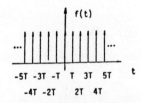

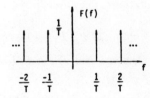

c. Periodic Impulses

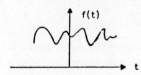

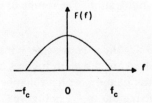

d. Random Functions

Figure 6.4. Common Time Domain Functions and Spectra

transformed into the frequency domain, the equivalent multiplication operation is convolution. That is,

$$f_1(t) \cdot f_2(t) = F_1(f) * F_2(f) \tag{6.4}$$

where $F_1(f)$ is the transform of $f_1(t)$ and the symbol * represents the convolution operation. If we can convolve F_1 and F_2, the resultant will be the transform of the sampler's output. This will illustrate the frequency content resulting from the sampling process and will provide insight into the phenomenon referred to as aliasing.

The convolution of F1 and F2 is expressed as

$$F_1(f) * F_2(f) = \int_{-\infty}^{\infty} F_1(\lambda) \, F_2(f - \lambda) \, d\lambda \tag{6.5}$$

Because λ is a complex variable, evaluation of the integral requires using residue theory. For our purposes, graphical interpretation of the convolution process is adequate to illustrate the sampling process.

6.2.4 A Graphical Approach to Convolution

The convolution process described above can be considered to consist of four operations. They are:

1. Folding of F_2: $F_2(-\lambda)$ is the mirror image of $F_2(\lambda)$

2. Displacement of F_2: $F_2(-\lambda)$ is shifted by an amount equal to f yielding $F_2(f-\lambda)$

3. Multiplication: The folded, displaced function $F_2(f-\lambda)$ is multiplied by $F_1(f)$

4. Integration: The results of steps 1 through 3 are summed from $-\infty$ to ∞.

To illustrate the process, consider Figure 6.5 where the functions to be convolved are shown in Figures 6.5a and 6.5b. For convenience in the graphical interpretation, we have numbered the pulses of the function F_2 and labeled the two regions of F_1. In Figure 6.5c, F_2 has been folded and superimposed on F_1. In Figure 6.5d, F_2 has been displaced an amount equal to $f_s/2$. In doing this, pulse number 3 has swept out region b of F_1. The product and summation is shown in Figure 6.5d as the shaded region. In Figure 6.5e, F_2 has been displaced an additional amount equal to $f_s/2$. During this time, pulse 4 has swept region a of F_1 creating the second shaded region. Continuing this process to infinity creates the spectrum shown in Figure 6.5f. Here, the convolved signal is seen to include the original F_1 spectrum plus an infinite number of sidelobes, each centered about the spectra of F_2. The infinite sidelobes (Figure 6.5f) confirm our suspicions that there is not a unique relationship between sampled data and the unsampled function.

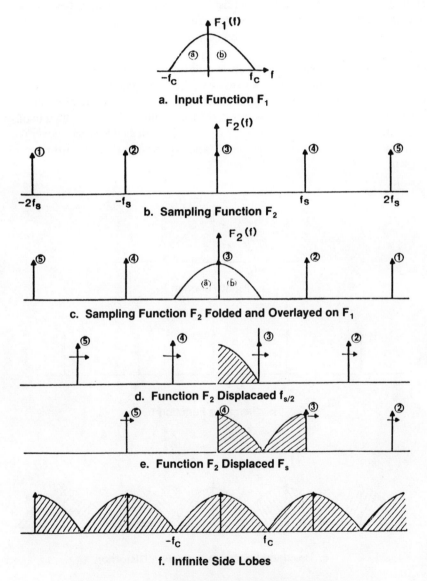

a. Input Function F_1

b. Sampling Function F_2

c. Sampling Function F_2 Folded and Overlayed on F_1

d. Function F_2 Displacaed $f_{s/2}$

e. Function F_2 Displaced F_s

f. Infinite Side Lobes

Figure 6.5. Convolution Using Graphical Techniques

If we had chosen f_s to be less than $2f_c$, it is obvious that the sidelobes would overlap producing distortion. In Figure 6.6, we illustrate this phenomenon for the previous functions. The functions F_1 and F_2 are shown in Figures 6.6a and b. Here, the sampling rate, f_s is chosen to be $1.5f_c$ rather than $2f_c$. In Figure 6.6c, we indicate the result of convolution. The distortion is illustrated by the cross-hatched areas. Based on on this, we can see that there is a relationship between f_s and f_c. In fact, the Nyquist sampling theorem states that a signal that is ideally band-limited can be constructed from impulse samples if the sampling rate is at least twice the highest (or cutoff) frequency. Thus, when $f_s \geq 2f_c$, no overlap occurs.

The spectra corresponding to an impulse sampled function consist of an infinite number of sidelobes. If we are concerned with analyzing sampled data, we must first choose a sampling frequency that is at least twice the cutoff frequency, and, second, we must process these sampled data through a band-pass filter whose window size is $-f_c < f < f_c$. This will enable us to recover the frequency information contained in F_1 and will ensure that no distortion is present.

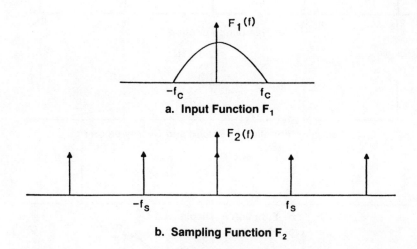

a. **Input Function F₁**

b. **Sampling Function F₂**

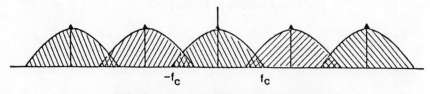

c. **Resulting Spectrum Indicating Distortion**

Figure 6.6. Distortion Resulting From Inadequate Sampling Rate

6.2.5 Non-Impulse Sampling

In discussing sampling thus far, we have assumed impulse sampling. This is typically done in describing the process and does not distort the presentation. However, in practice we know that converting from analog to digital does require a finite time, and thus the sampling pulses have non-zero width. Our sampling function consists of pulses of width τ repeated at a rate of T. The Fourier transform of this sampling function differs from that shown in Figure 6.5b in that the amplitude of the sampling pulses are not constant but rather diminish with frequency. The amplitude envelope is described by the following equation:

$$\text{Envelope} = \frac{\tau}{T} \quad \frac{\sin(\omega\tau/2)}{\omega\tau/2} \tag{6.6}$$

The frequency content of the resultant sampled signal would resemble that shown in Figure 6.5f but with each sidelobe diminished in amplitude.

6.3 TYPE I SAMPLING ERRORS

6.3.1 Sampling Interval

Type I Errors were defined as those errors attributable to sampling that affect amplitude accuracy. Assume that we have a system whose input can be represented as a sinusoidal of the form shown in Figure 6.7. Here, the system input can be expressed as:

$$f(t) = F_o + A \sin(\omega t) \tag{6.7}$$

where F_o is the average value, A is the peak amplitude of the sinusoidal, and ω is angular frequency.

Assume that for an input, such as illustrated in Figure 6.7, our interest is to define the extremes (i.e., the peak and minimum). Since we are going to represent this continuous signal with a set of discrete samples, it is unlikely that our samples will contain these extreme values. Our set of samples will, however, contain extremes. What error would be introduced if, for example, we elect to use the extreme values found in our sampled data set to represent the extremes of our input? Note that this is simply another way of asking how fast we must sample this input signal to ensure that we capture the extremes to within some tolerance.

One way of establishing sampling rate is to quantify the incremental change in the input function as a function of time. To a first approximation, we can do this using a simple point-slope expansion as shown in Figure 6.8. The incre-

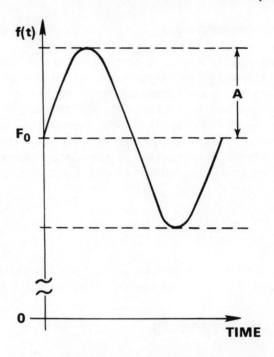

Figure 6.7. Input Sinusoidal

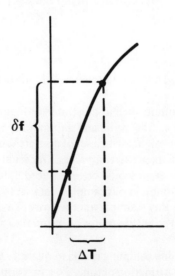

Figure 6.8. Point-Slope Expansion

mental change in the input function (denoted δf) that occurs in the time increment denoted ΔT can be approximated as follows:

$$\delta f = f'(t)\,\Delta T \tag{6.8}$$

where $f'(t)$ is the derivative and is equal to

$$f'(t) = \frac{df(t)}{dt} = \frac{d}{dt}\left[F_o + A\sin(\omega t)\right] \tag{6.9}$$

$$f'(t) = A\omega\cos(\omega t)$$

Thus, the change is

$$\delta f = \left[A\omega\cos(\omega t)\right]\Delta T \tag{6.10}$$

Since the magnitude of the cosine function can not exceed unity, then,

$$\delta f \leq A\omega\Delta T \tag{6.11}$$

If our objective is to choose a sampling time ΔT that will ensure that our samples are never more than δf apart, then we can use the above expression to determine ΔT.

According to the above discussion, one method of establishing sampling rate based on amplitude accuracy considerations is to quantify the amplitude change, δf, which will occur during the sampling time ΔT. To do this, we must know the input signal frequency and the magnitude of these variations. With this information and by assuming that the input is sinusoidal, we can determine a sampling frequency that will ensure that the amplitude error is less than a prescribed error.

Selecting sampling rate based on the above amplitude criteria places significant stress on the sampling rate. Using Equation 6.11, we can determine that if our allowable change, δf, is 1 percent of the peak amplitude A, then the required sampling rate is 100ω. While this approach is unreasonable and for most instances impractical, it does clearly indicate the following:

- The Nyquist sampling criteria of $2f_s$ is not sufficient to describe a waveform's character.

- The number of samples required to define a waveform's character depends upon how the data are to be analyzed as well as on the accuracy criteria.

6.3.2 Aperture Time

There are two keywords in the sampling theorem. First, the signal must be band-limited and second, the signal must be impulse-sampled. Both present difficult practical problems. As discussed previously, failure to provide band limiting introduces distortion as a consequence of frequency folding. This can be minimized by using a presampler filter (termed anti-aliasing filter) with sharp cut-off characteristics in conjunction with selecting a sampling rate at least twice as high as the effective signal bandwidth. The second consideration results from the fact that samplers are not ideal; that is, a finite time is required to sample the signal (Figure 6.9) and hence the signal is not impulse-sampled. Since our input is constantly changing, our concern is with how this conversion time affects amplitude accuracy. The following technique can be used to determine aperture time.

For sinusoidal inputs, the change that occurs during the time $\Delta\tau$ can be approximated using Equation 6.10 as follows:

$$\delta f = [A\omega\cos(\omega t)]\Delta\tau$$

To pick the worst case (i.e., the points where the δf function is at a maximum), we apply max-min theory. The δf function is at an extremum when the first derivative, $\delta f'$, is zero. Thus,

$$\delta f' = [-(\omega)A\omega\sin(\omega t)]\Delta\tau = 0 \tag{6.12}$$

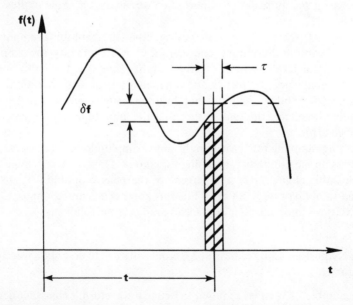

Figure 6.9. Effect of Finite Conversion (Aperture) Time on Amplitude Accuracy

implies for the nontrivial case that $\sin(\omega t) = 0$. Thus, the function is at an extremum when $\omega t = 0$, π, 2π, ..., $n\pi$. For these values of ωt, the absolute value of $\cos(\omega t)$ is one. Thus,

$$\delta f = A\omega\Delta\tau$$

which is what we determined previously.

We can use the above expression to define an upper limit for $\Delta\tau$. To do this, we must establish an acceptable value that the function can change. One way is to specify that the change must be less than or equal to the converter's resolution. Thus, if we are using an n-bit (excluding sign) converter whose full scale input is B, we can establish conversion time $\Delta\tau$ as follows:

$$\Delta\tau = \frac{\text{Converter Resolution, } V}{A\omega}$$

$$\Delta\tau = \frac{B}{A\omega 2^n}$$

(6.13)

6.4 TYPE II SAMPLING ERRORS

6.4.1 Concept of Frequency Distortion

While amplitude accuracy is important, we are oftentimes concerned with analyzing some function of time to determine its frequency content and to quantify the energy level at each discrete frequency. Improper sampling for this type of application can produce erroneous and misleading results. For example, if we fail to sample at a sufficiently high rate, we can be misled into thinking that our input function contains energy at nonexistent frequencies. Additionally, energy at real frequencies can vanish.

To illustrate this concept, consider the complex waveform of Figure 6.10. Here, the waveform is the sum of three different sinusoidals — each of which has a different amplitude. Our concern is in establishing a sampling rate such that there are no distortion errors (Type II Error).

If we perform a Fourier transform on the waveform of Figure 6.10, we can establish the spectra shown in Figure 6.11. From this, we determine that there is no energy past 5 hertz. Application of the Nyquist Sampling Theorem for this band-limited signal yields a sampling frequency of 10 hertz (i.e., $f_s = 2f_c$). Figure 6.12 illustrates the resultant spectra with infinite sidelobes. When we analyze data such as these, we would exclude these extraneous higher frequencies. Note that for the frequency range of interest, we have not introduced any distortion. That is, we are able to recover the 2-, 3-, and 5-hertz frequencies at the proper amplitudes.

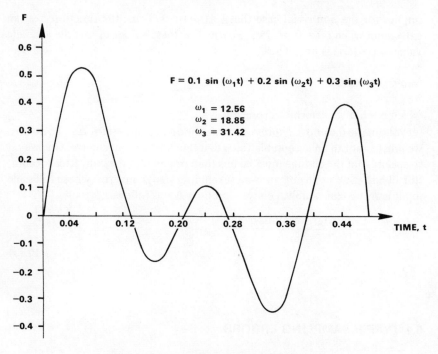

Figure 6.10. Complex Input Waveform

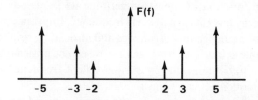

Figure 6.11. Spectra Corresponding to Figure 6.10

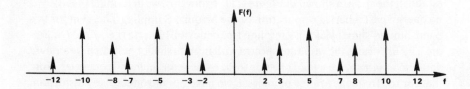

Figure 6.12. Sampled Resultant Spectra with Infinite Sidelobes

For the above case, we determined the frequency content (at least the highest frequency) and chose a sampling frequency based on this. Generally, we don't know the frequency content and thus aren't able to easily determine the sampling rate. To illustrate this, assume that we did not know the frequency content of the waveform illustrated in Figure 6.10 and mistakenly chose a sampling rate of 6 hertz. (For this example, we have assumed for computational convenience that all frequencies have the same amplitude.) The resultant sampled spectra are shown in Figure 6.13. Comparison of these to the sampled spectra illustrated in Figure 6.12 reveals several differences. First, the 3-hertz signal has vanished. Secondly, there appears to be energy present at both 1 and 4 hertz. In the time domain, this states that the two complex waveforms f_1 and f_2 defined by Equations 6.14 and 6.15 below are identical at the times defined by $1/6$ hertz.

$$f_1(t) = \sin(2 \cdot 2\pi \cdot t) + \sin(3 \cdot 2\pi \cdot t) + \sin(5 \cdot 2\pi \cdot t) \tag{6.14}$$

$$f_2(t) = \sin(1 \cdot 2\pi \cdot t) + \sin(2 \cdot 2\pi \cdot t) + \sin(4 \cdot 2\pi \cdot t) + \sin(5 \cdot 2\pi \cdot t) \tag{6.15}$$

The above illustrates the distortion that can be introduced through improper sampling. Unfortunately, there is no way to detect or eliminate these types of errors from sampled data. The solution lies with choosing the correct sampling rate in accordance with the Sampling Theorem based on the frequency content of the incoming signal.

6.4.2 Infinite Sidelobes

Based on the above discussion, we know that an analysis of these sampled data in the frequency domain will produce the input function as well as an infinite number of sidelobes. If we were careful in selecting the sampling rate, f_s, in conjunction with the input function's cutoff frequency, f_c, then we can determine the exact frequency content of the incoming signal. That is, there will be no distortion. To eliminate the sidelobes, we simply process the results of the frequency analysis through a software-implemented low pass filter whose cutoff frequency is less than or equal to $f_s/2$. Figure 6.14 illustrates this process.

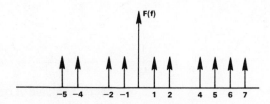

Figure 6.13. Improperly Sampled Resultant Spectra with Distortion

6.4.3 Filter Rolloff Rate Considerations

Properly filtering the input signal before quantization is necessary to ensure that no distortion in the frequency domain is present. Whereas we seldom know the input function's frequency content because of possible noise contamination, it is essential that we predetermine the range of frequencies that are of interest and establish a cutoff frequency, f_c. The objective is to choose a sampling rate, f_s, that will provide assurance that the frequencies between zero and f_c are not distorted. That is, no frequencies vanished, no aliases are present, and the amplitudes are accurate representations of the input signal.

The Sampling Theorem states that the input signal to the sampler must be band-limited. Accordingly, it is critical that we establish the frequency f_c^* beyond which there is no energy and use f_c^* to establish the sampling frequency f_s as follows:

$$f_s \geq 2f_c^*$$

Assuming that we do not know the incoming function's bandwidth, the designer's task is to limit the bandwidth by establishing f_c^* based on f_c.

Consider the function illustrated in Figure 6.15a, which has energy at frequencies extending to f_c^*. If we choose a sampling rate of f_s such that $f_s = 2f_c^*$, the resulting sampled spectra will appear as shown in Figure 6.15b. As shown, no distortion is present. However, based on an analysis of the experiment to be

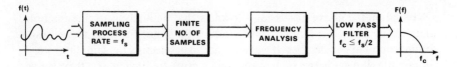

Figure 6.14. Low Pass Filtering Required to Eliminate Sidelobes

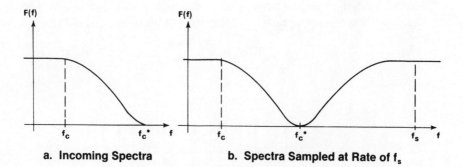

Figure 6.15. Relationship Between f_c, f_c^*, and f_s

conducted, we have predetermined that we are only interested in frequencies that extend to f_c. Since we will use a software implemented low pass filter to process the results of our frequency analysis, distortion at frequencies greater than f_c is acceptable. Accordingly, we can decrease the sampling rate such that distortion begins at f_c, which provides less stress on sampling rate. This is illustrated in Figure 6.16.

If we know f_c and f_c^*, we can establish the sampling frequency f_s as follows:

$$f_s \geq 2f_n$$

where f_n is the folding frequency. For applications such as that illustrated in Figure 6.16 where we want to ensure that no distortion occurs in the frequency range that extends to f_c, we can compute the folding frequency as follows:

$$\log f_n = \log f_c + \left(\frac{\log f_c^* - \log f_c}{2} \right)$$

$$\log f_n = \tfrac{1}{2} (\log f_c + \log f_c^*) \tag{6.16}$$

Accordingly, the sampling frequency is:

$$f_s \geq 2f_n \tag{6.17}$$

The variable's natural rolloff rate is normally not adequate to establish a reasonable f_c^*. Accordingly, a low pass filter is implemented in hardware prior to the sampler. Functionally, the filter is used to limit the bandwidth and thus is referred to as an anti-aliasing filter. With regard to Type II Sampling Error, the single most important filter characteristic is rolloff rate since it is used to establish f_c^*. Admittedly, phase, passband ripple, breakpoint characteristics, and overshoot are important. However, they do not affect sampling error.

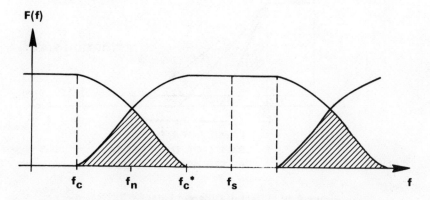

Figure 6.16. Sampled Spectrum Illustrating Distortion and Sidelobes

A conservative approach to use in establishing f_c^* is to assume the input function contains energy at all frequencies (Figure 6.17). If we process this through a low pass filter whose breakpoint is f_c and whose rolloff rate is defined, then the filter output contains energy extending to f_c^*. As shown in Figure 6.18, there is a family of f_c^* based on different filter rolloff rates. Since f_c^* is used to determine sampling rate f_s, there obviously is a tradeoff between filter rolloff and sampling rate.

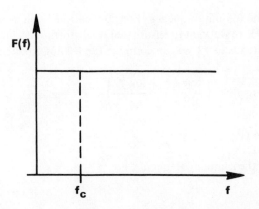

Figure 6.17. Input Function Contains Energy at All Frequencies

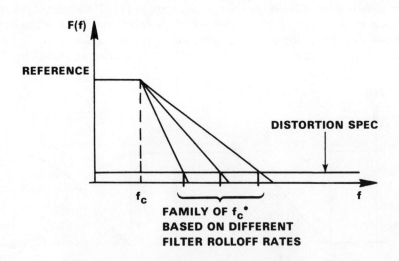

Figure 6.18. Effect of Different Filter Rolloff Rates on Effective Cutoff Frequency, f_c^*

6.4.4 Establishing f_c^* and f_s Using Converter Dynamic Range

The amplitude level we use to define f_c^* can be based on the sampler's resolution. That is, if we have an n-bit converter (excluding sign), the dynamic range of the converter can be expressed as:

$$\text{Dynamic Range, dB} = 20 \log (2^n) \tag{6.18}$$

We can use this to define f_c^* since any distortion at levels less than this can not be detected by the n-bit converter. The number of octaves required to achieve an attenuation level equal to the converter's dynamic range for a given filter is:

$$N = \frac{\text{Dynamic Range, dB}}{\text{Filter Rolloff Rate, dB/octave}} \tag{6.19}$$

This can be used to establish normalized cutoff frequency according to the following relationship:

$$\frac{f_c^*}{f_c} = \log^{-1} [N \log (2)] \tag{6.20}$$

Folding frequency, f_n, can then be established using Equation 6.16 as:

$$f_n = \log^{-1} (\tfrac{1}{2} \log f_c^*)$$

Finally, sampling rate is:

$$f_s \geq 2f_n$$

Figure 6.19 illustrates the relationship between normalized frequency and converter dynamic range for several different filter rolloff rates.

6.4.5 Establishing f_c^* and f_s Using Distortion Specifications at f_c

Using the converter's resolution to establish effective cutoff frequency f_c^* places significant stress on sampling frequency f_s. An alternative method is to specify an acceptable distortion at f_c. For example, consider the sampled function illustrated in Figure 6.20. Here, a distortion specification has been established based on a maximum allowable distortion at f_c. Graphically, we establish the effective cutoff frequency (denoted here as f_c^{**}) by the intersection of the filter's rolloff and the distortion specification line. Any energy present between f_c^{**} and f_c^* will appear as passband distortion.

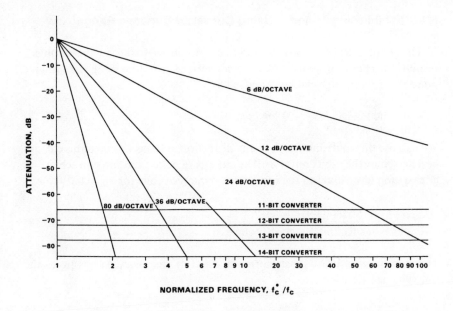

Figure 6.19. Establishing f_c^* with Different Filter Rolloff Rates

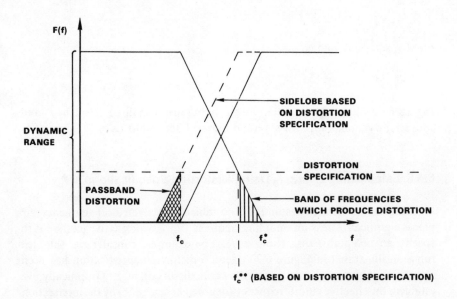

Figure 6.20. Establishing f_c^{**} Based on f_c Distortion Specification

Figure 6.21 illustrates the relationship between normalized sampling frequency and dynamic distortion error. Here the distortion specification is expressed as a percent of full scale at f_c. If we are willing to accept a maximum possible distortion at f_c of 1 percent, our sampling rate for a system employing a 12 dB/octave filter would be approximately 6.5. If this distortion specification is relaxed to 5 percent, the sampling rate can be reduced to approximately 4.5. It should be emphasized that if there is no energy present between f_c^{**} and f_c^*, there will not be any distortion.

6.5 FINALIZING THE SAMPLING/FILTERING DECISION

Based on our discussions thus far, we can conclude that determining how fast to sample is not a trivial exercise. While there are various technical and nontechnical considerations, the most significant of these is the tradeoff between filter rolloff characterisitcs and sampling frequency. In establishing these specifications, we considered the measurement's incoming frequency content and required bandwidth, the static accuracy, and frequency distortion. Although we attempted to categorize errors attributable to sampling according to static amplitude error and frequency distortion, we determined that the aliasing phenomena can produce errors at zero frequency. This is perhaps one of the most misunderstood error sources of all. Before we finalize our decision regarding sampling and filtering, we need to consider other technical aspects of the filter as well as practical sampling rate considerations.

6.5.1 Other Considerations Regarding the Filter

In our discussions thus far, we have considered the filter as ideal. That is, we considered that the amplitude characteristics within the passband were flat (i.e., zero insertion loss with no ripple) and that there was a discontinuity in amplitude that occurred precisely at the breakpoint. Additionally, we never considered phase distortion, transient characteristics, or settling time. For completeness, we include a discussion regarding these characteristics for the filters commonly offered by manufacturers. These typically are limited to Butterworth, Chebyshev, and Bessel. While the Elliptic or Cauer filters are available from a limited number of manufacturers, they are less commonly used as a consequence of their poor cost-to-performance characteristics. Table 6.1 summarizes the characteristics for the common filters in use.

As a consequence of both the filter's passband amplitude and phase characteristics, it may be necessary to position the filter's breakpoint at a frequency greater than the desired cutoff so as to achieve the desired characteristics. While this may provide desired amplitude and phase performance, it does penalize the sampling frequency.

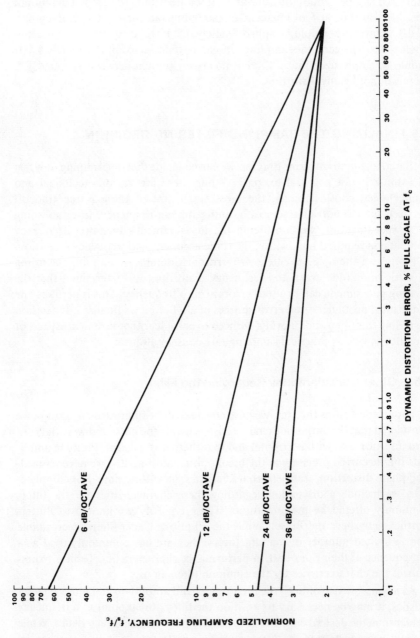

Figure 6.21. Relationship Between Sampling Frequency and Distortion Error at f$_c$ For Different Filter Rolloff Rates

Table 6.1. Summary of Filter Characteristics

FILTER TYPE	TYPICAL APPLICATION	REMARKS
BUTTERWORTH	AMPLITUDE RESPONSE WHERE PHASE IS NOT IMPORTANT	FLAT PASSBAND, POOR TRANSIENT CHARACTERISTICS
CHEBYSHEV	SIMILAR TO BUTTERWORTH	PASSBAND RIPPLE OF 0.01 - 0.5 dB POOR TRANSIENT CHARACTERISTICS
BESSEL	TRANSIENT MEASUREMENTS WHERE PHASE AND OVERSHOOT ARE CRITICAL	LINEAR PHASE, FLAT TIME DELAY, ZERO OVERSHOOT
ELLIPTIC	SPECTRUM SHAPING	PASSBAND AND STOPBAND RIPPLE, POOR PHASE, HIGH OVERSHOOT

[handwritten margin notes: "rings in response to step input", "good for processes with high dynamic content"]

6.5.2 Compromising Measurement Accuracy by Improper Sampling

If the system designer is not involved with establishing and enforcing software performance specifications, then it is possible that the required sampling rate will be unknowingly compromised. For many real-time applications, the processor is required to perform numerous functions such as engineering unit conversion, limit checks, displays, and closed-loop supervisory control in addition to data acquisition. Typically, the software designer is more concerned with creating a logical framework in which these functions may be implemented. As such, little or no attention is given to sampling rates. Instead, timing is based on a specification relating to display refreshes or else to the time required to detect an out-of-limit process condition and take action.

As we have discussed, improper sampling can create measurement errors. Unfortunately, errors such as those resulting from aliasing may never be detected. If they are detected, then they significantly impact application software. Because of the significant impact of high sampling rates on overall system performance, we would advocate biasing the filter/sampling rate analysis such that the minimum realizable sampling rate is chosen.

Example 6.1

Problem Statement

More often than not, we associate aliasing error simply with frequency and tend to discount this as a possible error for those applications where our interest is in the time domain rather than the frequency domain. Improper sampling, however, can introduce a zero frequency offset, thus affecting time domain analysis.

Determine the effects of improperly sampling an input that is described by the following equation

$$F(t) = F_o + \sin(\omega_1 t) + \sin(\omega_2 t)$$

where $\omega_1 = 12.56$, $\omega_2 = 18.85$. For computational convenience, we let $F_o = 0$.

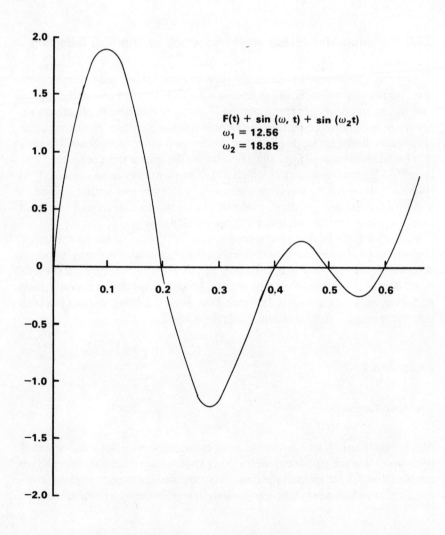

Solution

If we examine $F(t)$ in the frequency domain, we see that $F(f)$ consists of discrete frequencies of equal amplitude at 2 and 3 hertz. A simple sketch of the input function in the time domain and application of graphical convolution clearly illustrates that distortion will occur at zero frequency if the sampling frequency is not greater than 3 hertz. It is instructive to look at this in the time domain.

If we sample $F(t)$ at a rate greater than 3 hertz, we will conclude that our set of samples consists of both positive and negative values whose average is zero. The table below contains data sampled at 4, 5 and 6 Hz. A cursory analysis indicates that a one-second average for each case is zero.

$f_s = 4$ Hz		$f_s = 5$ Hz		$f_s = 6$ Hz	
TIME	**SAMPLE**	**TIME**	**SAMPLE**	**TIME**	**SAMPLE**
0.35	−0.64	0.1	1.90	0.1$\bar{6}$	0.86
0.60	0	0.3	−1.17	0.3$\bar{3}$	−0.86
0.85	−1.27	0.5	0	0.50	0
1.10	+1.90	0.7	1.18	0.6$\bar{6}$	0.86
1.35	−0.64	0.9	−1.90	0.8$\bar{3}$	−0.86
1.60	0	1.1	1.90	1.0	0
1.85	−1.26	1.3	−1.17	1.1$\bar{6}$	0.86
2.10	+1.90	1.5	0	1.3$\bar{3}$	−0.86

If we sample the data at a rate less than or equal to 3 Hz, the sampled data will all have the same sign, thus providing a non-zero offset. The table below indicates the results of sampling at rates of 2 and 3 hertz.

fs = 3 Hz		fs = 2 Hz	
TIME	**SAMPLE**	**TIME**	**SAMPLE**
0.4$\bar{3}$	0.21	0.1	1.9
0.7$\bar{6}$	0.75	0.6	0
1.0$\bar{9}$	1.89	1.1	1.9
1.4$\bar{3}$	0.20	1.6	0
1.7$\bar{6}$	0.75		
2.10	1.89		
AVG = 0.95		**AVG = 0.95**	

From this simple example, we see that aliasing does introduce an amplitude error (at zero frequency). Regardless of the number of samples we use in establishing an average from improperly sampled data, the average will never be zero. Aliasing can thus compromise any amplitude accuracy improvements gained through high quality instrumentation.

Example 6.2

Problem Statement

Consider an application where the signals to be measured are contaminated with noise. If we are to utilize a sampled data system to measure analog voltages that have noise superimposed on them and if our intent is to quantify the static (average) value, we must filter or smooth the inputs such that one value will be representative of the average.

Consider the following function of time, which has noise superimposed on a static level.

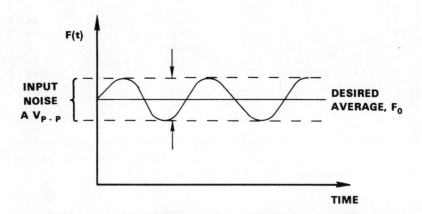

Through experimentation or as a stated requirement, we determine that the worst-case noise has a magnitude of A volts peak-to-peak and that the frequency is f_1. Note that if we apply this signal directly into a converter and if we take instantaneous samples to represent this function, we are going to observe scatter in the data.

For this example, the requirement is that the variation in observed data resulting from noise must be less than B volts peak-to-peak. In all likelihood, this will be stated in engineering units. Thus, we either need to know the input noise in engineering units or we must convert the requirement to voltage. In either case, both the input noise and the requirement on scatter must be in consistent units. The previous sketch is repeated below with the variation requirement of B volts peak-to-peak superimposed.

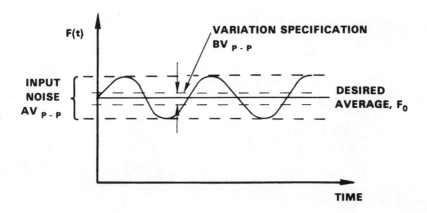

Design a passive low pass filter that will attenuate the input noise to an acceptable level. We require it to be a passive filter because the input levels are in the mV range. For this example, use the following data:

A = 1 V
B = 0.01 V
f_1 = 60 Hz

Solution

We can sketch the problem in the frequency domain as:

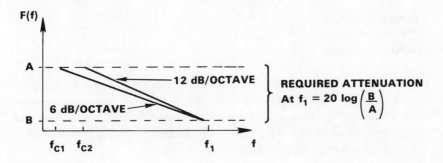

We are required to establish the filter rolloff rate and the corresponding breakpoint frequency, f_c. Since our interest is with steady-state measurements, there is no lower limit imposed on f_c. Since our filter must be passive, we only have two possible attenuation rates — 6 dB/octave and 12 dB/octave. Thus, the breakpoint frequency is either f_{c1} or f_{c2}. The required filter attenuation is:

$$\text{Attenuation} = 20 \log \left(\frac{B}{A} \right)$$

$$= -40 \text{ dB}$$

The number of octaves between f_1 and f_c is:

- 6 dB/octave filter

- $N = \dfrac{\text{Attenuation, dB}}{\text{Filter Attenuation, dB}}$

  $N = 6.\overline{6}$

- 12 dB/octave filter

  $N = 3.\overline{3}$

We determine the breakpoint frequency as:

- 6 dB/octave filter

  $f_c = f_1 \left(\log^{-1} [N \log(2)] \right)^{-1}$

  $= 60 \text{ Hz} \left(\log^{-1} [6.6 \log(2)] \right)^{-1}$

  $= 0.59 \text{ hertz}$

- 12 dB/octave filter

  $f_c = 5.95 \text{ hertz}$

Example 6.3

Problem Statement

Given an input consisting of two discrete frequencies, f_1 and f_2, of equal magnitudes where f_2 is considered to be unwanted noise, determine the sampling frequency such that f_1 contains no more than 5 percent distortion and verify the results. For this example, use a 12-dB/octave filter with breakpoint at f_1 of 1 hertz and let f_2 equal 4.5 hertz.

Solution

We want the passband to be flat to 1 Hz and to attenuate the noise ($f_2 = 4.5$ Hz) such that if aliased, f_2 will not distort f_1 by more than 5 percent.

1. Determine octaves required from f_1 to cutoff frequency f_c^*.

$$N = \frac{26 \text{ dB}}{12 \text{ dB/octave}} = 2.168$$

Here the effective cutoff frequency, f_c^*, is defined as 4.5 Hz since we are not interested in data beyond 1 Hz.

2. Determine folding frequency.

$$f_n = \log^{-1}(\tfrac{1}{2} \log f_c^*) = 2.12 \text{ Hz}$$

3. Determine sampling frequency.

$$f_s = 2f_n = 4.24 \text{ Hz}$$

We can verify the results by sampling the following function at the frequency established above.

$$f(t) = \sin(\omega_1 t) + A \sin(\omega_2 t)$$

where $\omega_1 = 6.28$, $\omega_2 = 28.3$ and $A = 0.05$. The data are tabulated below for $f_2 = 4.5$ Hertz and $f_2 = 0$. Comparison of the function values indicates a magnitude difference of 5 percent.

$f_2 = 4.5$ Hz		$f_2 = 0$	
TIME	**f(t)**	**TIME**	**f(t)**
0	0	0	0
0.1	0.60	0.1	0.59
0.2	0.92	0.2	0.95
0.3	0.99	0.3	0.95
0.4	0.54	0.4	0.59
0.5	0.05	0.5	0
0.6	−0.63	0.6	−0.59
0.7	−0.91	0.7	−0.95
0.8	−0.98	0.8	−0.95
0.9	−0.57	0.9	−0.59
1.0	0	1.0	0

Example 6.4

Problem Statement

Consider an application where time invariant variables are to be measured. Although the desired bandwidth for this application is generally considered to be near zero, it is typically specified as 2–10 Hz to provide reasonable response for transient conditions. For such an application, let a typical input be described by the following equation:

$$F(t) = \tau \dot{m} + m + A \sin(\omega t)$$

where m is the measurement, $\dot{m}$ is the time rate of change, and τ is the measurement's time constant. The term $A \sin(\omega t)$ represents an unwanted noise component attributable to line frequency with $\omega = 377$. Determine the effects of the noise component on static accuracy for an application where the filter's rolloff rate is 12 dB/octave, $f_c = 10$ Hz, and the peak magnitude of electrical noise is 50 mV.

Solution

Determine the noise attenuation provided by the 12 dB/octave filter.

1. Number of octaves:

$$\frac{f_c^*}{f_c} = \log^{-1}[N \log(2)]$$

For $f_c^* = 60$ Hz, $f_c = 10$ Hz

$$N = \frac{\log(6)}{\log(2)} = 2.58$$

2. Noise attenuation:

Attenuation = (N) (Filter Rolloff Rate)

= –31 dB

3. Attenuated Noise Magnitude

$$dB = 20 \log$$
$$e_o = (0.028)e_1$$
$$= 1.4 \text{ mV}$$

Thus, the 50 mV peak electrical noise will appear as 1.4 mV peak. To determine the equivalent error, the system's gain and analog-to-digital converter's characteristics must be considered. Note: Line frequency noise can introduce significant measurement errors for these sensors that have mV outputs.

Chapter 7
Functional Design

7.1 INTRODUCTION

The process of going from a user's stated want or need to a set of procurement specifications and build documents is termed **engineering design**. To separate the initial conceptual design phase from that part involved with the intimate details, we oftentimes discuss system design in terms of Functional Design and Final Design. Functional design is considered to be those activities that establish the form of the solution (i.e., front-end and processor configuration and characteristics), whereas final design is considered to encompass the implementation related activities (i.e., how are things connected).

With this definition, final design is considered to be an expansion of, or to build upon, the results of functional design. Consequently, functional design is considered to be the most critical activity in the design process. During this phase, decisions are made that affect technical adequacy, cost, and schedule. As used here, functional design encompasses all tasks required to translate requirements into a system configuration and to develop performance and functional specifications for both hardware and software. At the completion of functional design, we are able to establish reasonable estimates of both cost and schedule. More fundamentally, we are able at this point in the design process to state whether or not the requirements are economically and technically realizable.

To safeguard against the phenomenon known as creeping eloquence, which plagues most ill-defined systems during final design, thus resulting in increased costs and missed schedules, it is essential that functional design provide a sound technical basis for final design. By this, we mean that all elements of the system that affect cost and performance and require detailing must be clearly defined. Additionally, each attribute of the functional design must be related to the requirements if we are to achieve required performance at minimum cost. Thus, the designer must be able to either relate the specifications and configuration to requirements through sound analysis techniques or to technically justify decisions based on cost-to-performance tradeoff studies.

We can obtain an insight into the areas that we should consider important for functional design by considering those elements of a system that significantly affect either cost or performance. Thus, we are concerned with the context in which the system is to be used and with measurement characteristics such as accuracy, numbers and types of inputs, bandwidths, and processing capabilities. We are also concerned with the environment in which the system must operate, space constraints, maintenance and operation, reliability, and cost.

Figure 7.1 illustrates an overview of the functional design process. For simplicity, the analyses are shown as three separate and parallel activities — accuracy, bandwidth, and performance. In reality, the analyses are not independent but instead are highly coupled, indicating that they may not be conducted in isolation but rather must be coordinated by a systems engineer. The results from these analyses are used by the systems engineer in conjunction with other miscellaneous requirements and constraints to establish the system configuration and performance specifications for both hardware and software. As we stated previously, the attributes of the system should be checked at this point in the process against the requirements to ensure completeness. If the attributes cannot be justified, either the requirements must be changed or the attributes in question deleted. Not only is this necessary to ensure that stated requirements are realized at minimal cost, it is critical to safeguard against creeping eloquence if the primary system requirements are to be completed in a timely manner. The analyses, configuration, and specifications — along with documented evidence that these have been checked by an independent systems engineer who has concluded that these results are traceable, technically correct, and that if implemented they will satisfy the requirements — form the basis for detail design.

Once we have addressed all requirements and established a system configuration and specifications, the design should be placed under configuration control. By this, we mean a mechanism is implemented whereby any change in requirements that occurs during final design cannot be incorporated without formal approval. For approval, each change request must be analyzed and its impact on both cost and schedule documented.

In the remainder of this chapter, we review individually the different analyses that are required (accuracy, bandwidth, performance) before we establish the system configuration.

7.2 ACCURACY

Much has been said in previous chapters about measurement accuracy, and rightly so. Since one of the system's primary objectives is to make measurements and provide information, we consider this a fundamental design criterion and seek analytical techniques that relate individual system component accuracy to overall measurement accuracy. We summarize the technique in the following subsections.

7.2.1 Individual Measurement Error

As shown in Figure 7.1, information relationships may be parametric. That is, the information relationships may involve combining several measurements mathematically. This can be stated as:

$$F_i = f_i(m_1, m_2, \ldots, m_n) \tag{7.1}$$

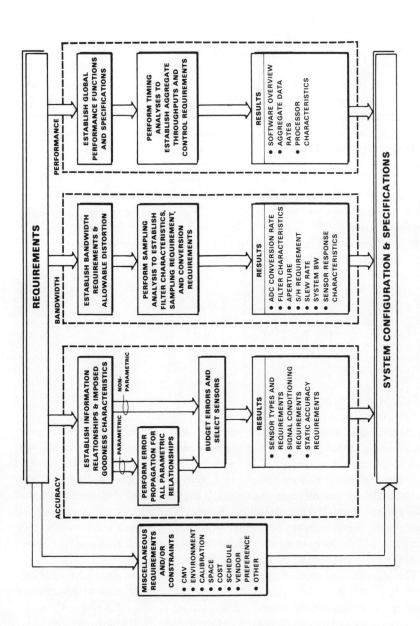

Figure 7.1. Overview of Functional Design Process

where F_i is the information relationship and the m_j are measurements. If we impose a goodness requirement, which we denote δF_i, on this relationship at a set of conditions, we can expand the function in a Taylor series to establish the following relationship:

$$a_1 \Delta m_1 + a_2 \Delta m_2 + \ldots + a_n \Delta m_n = C \tag{7.2}$$

where a_j are the partial derivatives evaluated at the stated conditions, C is the goodness requirement, and Δm_j are the individual measurement errors. Applying the RSS yields the following nonlinear relationship between the measurement error and goodness specification, which is valid for the function F_i only at the conditions where the partials were evaluated:

$$(a_1 \Delta m_1)^2 + (a_2 \Delta m_2)^2 + \ldots + (a_n \Delta m_n)^2 = C^2 \tag{7.3}$$

For this relationship, we can choose values for $n - 1$ of the Δm_i and solve for the remaining value.

If our requirements involve multiple relationships, we apply this technique to each and establish the following system of equations:

$$
\begin{bmatrix}
a_{11}^2 & a_{12}^2 & \cdots & a_{1n}^2 \\
a_{21}^2 & a_{22}^2 & \cdots & a_{2n}^2 \\
\cdot \\
\cdot \\
\cdot \\
a_{m1}^2 & a_{m2}^2 & \cdots & a_{mn}^2
\end{bmatrix}
\begin{bmatrix}
\Delta m_1^2 \\
\Delta m_2^2 \\
\\
\\
\Delta m_n^2
\end{bmatrix}
=
\begin{bmatrix}
C_1^2 \\
C_2^2 \\
\\
\\
C_n^2
\end{bmatrix}
\tag{7.4}
$$

As shown, it is likely that a given measurement may be used with different relationships. Consequently, we cannot view each relationship individually but must consider them collectively.

A word of caution about the above system of equations. Each row of the $m \times n$ coefficient matrix consists of partials that have been evaluated at a set of steady-state measurement conditions. Since it is unlikely that the same set of steady-state measurement conditions will apply for each relationship, this approach, which strives to establish Δm_i to satisfy multiple relationships, is not generally valid and should be viewed with caution.

The approach advocated requires simultaneously considering all relationships that involve one or more common measurements. We first group relationships involving common measurements. Each relationship is then solved to establish individual measurement errors that will satisfy that single relationship. The solutions are then collectively viewed and an error specification established for the common measurements that will satisfy all relationships.

As an example, consider an application involving three relationships that share at least one common measurement, m_i. Table 7.1 below focuses on the specifications relative to m_i for each relationship.

Table 7.1. Requirement Specifications Emphasizing Measurement m_i

Relationship	Range for m_i	Goodness Requirement
$F_1 = f(m_1, \ldots, m_i, \ldots, m_n)$	$m_i^1 \le m_i \le m_i^3$	C_1 at m_i^1, C_3 at m_i^3
$F_2 = f(m_1, \ldots, m_i, \ldots, m_n)$	$m_i^2 \le m_i \le m_i^4$	C_2 at m_i^2, C_4 at m_i^4
$F_3 = f(m_1, \ldots, m_i, \ldots, m_n)$	$m_i^2 \le m_i \le m_i^4$	C_2 at m_i^2, C_4 at m_i^4

Each relationship is solved to establish allowable errors for all measurements at each goodness requirement. Figure 7.2 illustrates this for the measurement m_i. As shown, our error specification for the measurement m_i over the range $m_i^1 \le m_i \le m_i^4$ is the minimum set of errors Δm_i.

The goodness requirements tabulated above for the three different functions and shown graphically in Figure 7.2 are based on measurement extremes for each function. Since there are no specifications to describe error in between end points, the designer may conclude that the end points for each function should be linearly connected. If this method is adopted, the character of the composite error specification will differ from that shown in Figure 7.2.

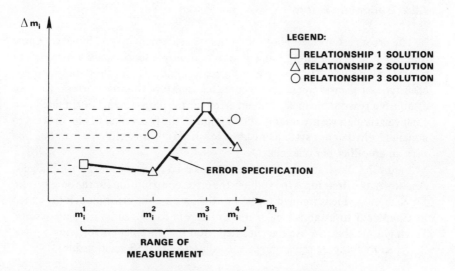

Figure 7.2. Error Specification For a Common Measurement
Established From Multiple Relationships

For each of the measurements m_i to be made, the above techniques will enable us to establish total error as either a single value Δm_i, which is applicable at either a specific value or over a range,

$$m_i^l \leq m_i \leq m_i^u \tag{7.5}$$

or as a set of values Δm_j, $j = 1, 2, \ldots, n$, which corresponds to the measured values m_j, $j = 1, 2, \ldots, n$. Since our system is to be a multichannel system and as such will be required to measure various phenomena, it is desirable from an error budgeting point of view that we nondimensionalize the errors by considering the errors in terms of either percent of full scale or percent of reading. There are, of course, some measurements, such as speeds and temperatures, that do not readily lend themselves to percentage conversion and are more easily dealt with in engineering units.

Figure 7.3 illustrates an overview of the analysis required in establishing our composite measurement list. As a minimum, the list should contain the following:

- List of all measurements and ranges

- Corresponding total measurement errors

Having quantified the total accuracy requirements, the next step in the process is to establish an error budget.

7.2.2 Budgeting Errors

The errors established above are total measurement errors. Since we know that our system as a minimum will require multiple sensors and a shared data system, it is desirable to first establish a reasonable error for the data system for each type of measurement and to use this to establish sensor errors. Can we establish a reasonable measurement error for the data system? Fortunately, we can even though we are unable at this point in the functional design process to conclude whether our system must be a low level multiplexed system or one that uses an amplifier per channel.

Figure 7.4 illustrates the iterative process used in establishing error budgets. As shown, the first step is to establish the error contribution for the data system for each of the measurement types. For this, we use the error models presented in Chapter 5 to establish measurement errors for a candidate data system. Having done this, we use the specified total measurement error (Δm_j, $j = 1$, $2, \ldots, n$) to compute sensor error according to the RSS relationship

$$\text{Sensor Error, } i = \pm \left[(\text{Specified Meas Error, } \Delta m_j)^2 - (\text{Data Sys Error})^2 \right]^{1/2}$$

$$\tag{7.6}$$

Using the computed sensor error, we next choose one or more sensors to cover the required range and satisfy the total measurement error specifications. Thus, for example, we may conclude that multiple pressure sensors, each with different ranges, are required to cover the entire range and to satisfy the measurement accuracy specifications. The final step involves computing the total measurement uncertainty using the chosen data system and sensor(s) and comparing this to the specifications. Based on this, some iteration may be required, or even some possible compromising of requirements.

A note of caution: While using multiple sensors, each of a different range, to make one measurement appears to be the answer to providing reasonable error

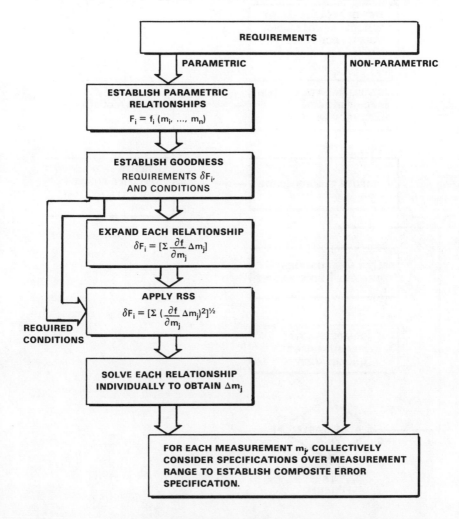

Figure 7.3. Analysis Required in Establishing Individual Measurement Error

over a broad range, it is not a panacea. The immediate concerns are possible overranging of sensors connected in parallel, measurement continuity at cross-over points, complexity, and cost. However, there may not be any alternative if the requirements are real.

There are variations with this budgeting technique. For example, if we have prior knowledge of measurement accuracy results for some of the more common measurement types, we can go immediately from measurement accuracy

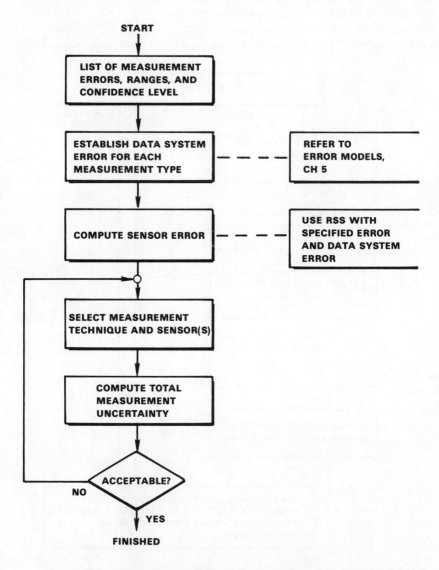

Figure 7.4. Establishing Error Budgets For Sensor and Data System

specifications to sensor selection. Table 7.2 summarizes the results of an error analysis partially presented in Chapter 5 that was conducted for several common measurements. The accuracies presented are considered to be representative of those achievable in 1985 with either low level multiplexed systems or with amplifier-per-channel multiplexed systems.

The data presented in Table 7.2 are of significant interest in that they clearly indicate the extreme difficulty of making absolutely accurate measurements. Thus, we see the following:

- The uncertainty associated with temperature measurements made using thermocouples is driven by the large bias error associated with the thermocouple.

- The measurement uncertainty of RTD's is driven not by the sensor or data system accuracy but by the way that the RTD is configured and by the mode of excitation. As it is with thermocouples, these large errors are biases that can be removed through careful calibration.

- There is no significant difference in measurement uncertainty for sensors that have internal signal conditioning as compared to those sensors that provide low level signal outputs. While not shown, there is a potential bias error associated with sensors that use internal signal conditioning and a grounded excitation supply. This error is the result of a CMV.

Comparison of the Sensor Uncertainty column of Table 7.2 to Total Measurement Uncertainty provides an insight into data system uncertainty. While not stated, quality data systems exhibit errors that typically are on the order of 0.1–0.2 percent of full scale.

7.2.3 Implications of Sensor Selection

The error budget technique allows us to tentatively select sensors based on an assumed data system performance. For example, with passive sensors we assumed an error contribution based on power supply performance, offset suppression, and common mode voltage. Now that a sensor has been chosen based on budgeted error, we need to reevaluate the magnitude of these errors and use this to establish specifications for the data system signal conditioning.

Figure 7.5 illustrates the technique for finalizing sensor selection that begins where the previous step (Budgeting Errors) ended. Thus, we start with a set of selected sensors and categorize them as either passive or active. Since passive sensors require excitation, we need to establish the effects of power supply variations on measurement error. For either type sensor, we are also concerned about signal conditioning such as bridge completion, offset suppression, temperature reference junction, effects of common mode voltage, and effects of

Table 7.2. Typical Sensor and Data System Measurement Uncertainties For Common Measurements

SENSOR TYPE	CONFIGURATION	RANGE	SENSOR UNCERTAINTY	TOTAL MEASUREMENT UNCERTAINTY
TYPE J T/C	STANDARD	32°F TO 530°F 530°F TO 1382°F	±4°F ±0.75% Rdg	±4.3°F ±10.4°F
TYPE K T/C	STANDARD	−328°F TO 530°F 530°F TO 2282°F	±4°F ±0.75% Rdg	±4.3°F ±17.4°F
TYPE T T/C	STANDARD	−328°F TO −266°F −266°F TO 530°F 530°F TO 662°F	±1.5% Rdg ±1.8°F ±0.75% Rdg	±5.2°F ±2.1°F ±5.3°F
TYPE J T/C	SPECIAL	32°F TO 500°F 500°F TO 1382°F	±2°F ±0.4% Rdg	±2.3°F ±5.8°F
TYPE K T/C	SPECIAL	32°F TO 500°F 500°F TO 2282°F	±2°F ±0.4% Rdg	±2.3°F ±9.4°F
TYPE T T/C	SPECIAL	32°F TO 225°F 225°F TO 662°F	±0.9°F ±0.4% Rdg	±1.2°F ±2.9°F
RTD △2	3-WIRE CONSTANT VOLTAGE	−250°F TO 250°F −328°F TO 1200°F	±(0.3% Rdg + 0.45°F) ±(0.3% Rdg + 0.45°F)	7.9°F 8.8°F
RTD △3	3-WIRE CONSTANT CURRENT	−250°F TO 250°F −328°F TO 1200°F	±(0.3% Rdg + 0.45°F) ±(0.3% Rdg + 0.45°F)	3.1°F 4.9°F
RTD △1	4-WIRE CONSTANT CURRENT	−250°F TO 250°F −328°F TO 1200°F	±(0.3% Rdg + 0.45°F) ±(0.3% Rdg + 0.45°F)	1.2°F 4.1°F
RTD - SPECIAL	3-WIRE CONSTANT CURRENT	−250°F TO 250°F −328°F TO 932°F	±(0.2% Rdg + 0.18°F) ±(0.2% Rdg + 0.18°F)	±2.9°F ±3.4°F
RTD - SPECIAL	4-WIRE CONSTANT CURRENT	−250°F TO 250°F −328°F TO 932°F	±(0.2% Rdg + 0.18°F) ±(0.2% Rdg + 0.18°F)	±0.7°F ±2.0°F
STRAIN GAGE	EXTERNAL CONDITIONING (3mV/V)	0-10K psi 0-10K psi	±0.20% FS ±0.75% FS	±0.22% FS ±0.88% FS
STRAIN GAGE	INTERNAL CONDITIONING (5V)	0-10K psi 0-10K psi	±0.20% FS ±0.75% FS	±0.21% FS ±0.88% FS
CAPACITANCE MANOMETER	BCD OUTPUT	0-10 mmHg 0-10,000 mmHg	±0.05% Rdg ±0.08% Rdg	±0.05% Rdg ±0.08% Rdg
CAPACITANCE MANOMETER	ANALOG OUTPUT	0-10 mmHg 0-10,000 mmHg	±0.05% Rdg ±0.08% Rdg	±0.12% FS ±0.15% FS

NOTES:

△1   TOTAL MEASUREMENT UNCERTAINTY IS ±3σ

△2   100 ohm RTD, LINE RESISTANCE OF 1.6 ohms, EXCITATION OF 10V

△3   100 ohm RTD, LINE RESISTANCE OF 1.6 ohms, EXCITATION OF 3mA

environment on the sensor. Throughout this process, our objective is to establish data system specifications (power supply, signal conditioning, CMRR, gains) based on a set of selected sensors that are consistent with the overall measurement accuracy requirements. If, in the process of evaluating the implications associated with the selected sensor, it is determined that the overall performance cannot be realized, a different sensor must be chosen and the process repeated. The following system characteristics or specifications should be established at the completion of this analysis.

7.2.3.1 Power Supply

Characteristics

- Mode: Constant Voltage and/or Constant Current
- Sense: Local, Remote
- Short Circuit Protection
- Current/Voltage Limiting

Specifications

- Output: Grounded, Floating
- Range: Volts and Current
- Regulation: Load, Line
- Noise
- Stability

7.2.3.2 Signal Conditioning

Characteristics

- Bridge Completion: Number of Arms
- Calibration: Resistive Shunt and/or Voltage Insertion
- Thermocouple Reference: Heated, Ambient

Specifications

- Offset Suppression: Range, Error
- Thermocouple Reference: Error

7.2.3.3 Amplifier

Characteristics

- Input: Single-Ended, Differential
- Gain: Range

Specifications

- CMV: Maximum Safe CMV, CMRR
- Input: Impedance
- Gain: Accuracy

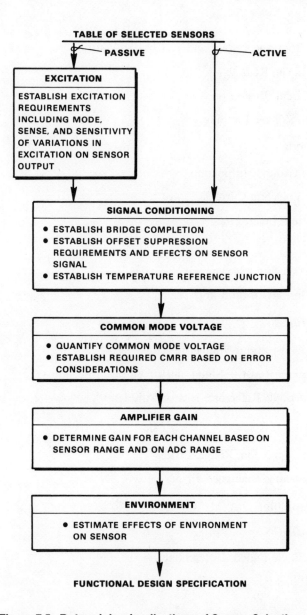

Figure 7.5. Determining Implications of Sensor Selection

7.3 BANDWIDTH

Establishing the measurement's bandwidth requirement is perhaps one of the most difficult tasks we are faced with in system design. It is difficult because of our reluctance to quantify the bandwidth needed for our application and because of the misunderstanding regarding sampling. Yet, bandwidth is one of the critical factors used in selecting sensors and in establishing measurement system specifications. Underestimating bandwidth can introduce significant distortion in the measurement, whereas overestimating bandwidth requirements can significantly impact the system's complexity and cost. How can we quantify bandwidth? To answer this, we need to determine why the measurement is being made. What will the data be used for? If our concern is with establishing the time averaged value of some phenomenon such as pressure or temperature, then bandwidth is not critical. In fact, underestimating bandwidth can help if our measurement is contaminated with high frequency noise. Thus, we might choose to use a temperature sensor with a relatively large thermal mass for a steady-state type of measurement. The sensor's time constant would average out any higher frequency temperature fluctuations that may be present (these high frequency fluctuations are considered noise and are unwanted if our objective is to establish an average value). On the other hand, if we were to use the temperature sensor as feedback in a closed-loop control loop, then our bandwidth concern is directly related to the process time constant. Incorrect time response for this application can lead to undesirable controller characteristics.

An accurate estimate of each measurement's bandwidth is important if our system is to provide the desired results. As illustrated in Figure 7.1, we need measurement bandwidth to aid us in establishing the following system characteristics:

- Sensor Response Characteristics
- ADC Conversion Rate
- Filter Characteristics
- Aperture
- Sample and Hold
- Amplifier Slew Rate

These key system attributes can be established or inferred from measurement bandwidth by analysis.

7.3.1 Sensor Response Characteristics

We should recognize that oftentimes the phenomenon to be measured is not stationary but varies with time. As an example, consider Figure 7.6, which illustrates a time varying phenomenon such as pressure. The variations shown may or may not be of interest. That is, they may simply be unwanted fluctuations that are the result of the process, or they may be a desirable measure of a disturbance. In the first case, the fluctuations represent a potential error source since a measurement can conceivably take on any value between P_1 and P_2 depending on time and the measurement technique. In the second case, an error may be introduced by the response of the measurement system. In either case, the variations represent a potential error source.

Based on the above discussion, we see that there are two types of measurements that may be of interest. If we are interested in only the quasi-stationary value of a measurement, we term the measurement **steady-state** and seek ways to minimize excursions. If our interest is the time history of a phenomenon, we term the measurement **dynamic** and attempt not to distort the measurement response. Although these terms are not industry standards, they are descriptive of the phenomenon to be measured.

Consider that the fluctuations shown in Figure 7.6 illustrate temperature variations in a fluid. If a thermal mass is inserted in the fluid, the temperature of the thermal mass will lag the fluid temperature. Similarly, if a pneumatic pressure transducer of finite volume is used to measure pressure fluctuations of similar character, the measured pressure will lag the applied pressure. The behavior of each of these systems can be approximated by a first-order differential equation.

Before proceeding, we need to emphasize that our purpose is not to rigorously derive relationships between the input and output of a measurement system. Rather, we seek simple means of approximating the response characteristics. Both heat transfer and pressure propagation are complex mechanisms. However, for our purposes, their response behavior can be approximated.

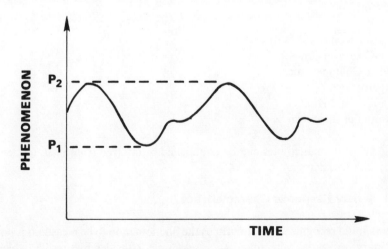

Figure 7.6. Typical Time Variation of Measurement Phenomenon

Consider the following linear first-order differential equation:

$$A\dot{m} + m = F(t) \tag{7.7}$$

where $\dot{m}$ represents the time rate of change of the measurement m, A is a non-negative constant, and $F(t)$ is an input forcing function. As shown, this is a linear first-order differential equation and as such has the following closed-form solution:

$$m = \frac{1}{A} \, e^{\frac{-t}{A}} \int F(t)e^{\frac{t}{A}} \, dt + ce^{\frac{-t}{A}} \tag{7.8}$$

As a special case, the solution can be given by the following:

$$m = F_0 + ce^{\frac{-t}{A}} \tag{7.9}$$

when $F(t)$ is a constant value F_0. For the constant input, it can be seen that as t approaches infinity, m approaches the constant F_0. After a transient period, the output agrees with the input.

From the above equation, it can be seen that the time required to reach the final value is a function of the constant A. Hence, A has the dimension of time and is appropriately called the **time constant**. When t equals A, m will have changed 63.2 percent of the difference between F_0 and F_1. When t equals $2A$, m will be within 86.5 percent. From this, it can be seen that m approaches F_0 exponentially but will never exactly equal F_0. However, for all practical purposes, m can be said to equal F_0 when time equals $5A$. We rely heavily on the concept of time constant when describing the response of measurement systems.

Quantifying sensor response analytically using manufacturer's literature is difficult to accomplish with any degree of certainty. This is largely because the response characteristics are significantly influenced by the application. For pressure measurements, we must be careful about selecting transducers whose volume and natural frequency are consistent with the required bandwidth. More importantly, we must be extremely careful about the installation (tubing lengths and diameters) if our concern is to preserve bandwidth. Similarly, the response of a temperature measurement is significantly influenced by both the method of heat transfer and the sensor's physical properties (mass, area, specific heat coefficient). We discuss each of these two measurements in general terms below.

7.3.1.1 Pneumatic Response

The response of a pneumatic system can be described under certain qualifying assumptions by the following equation:

$$K_m \dot{P}_m + P_m^2 = p^2 - K\dot{P} \tag{7.10}$$

where P_m is the measured pressure, P is the applied pressure, and both K_m and K are functions of the pneumatic geometry. If we replace the right-hand side by $F(P)$ and divide through P_m, then we obtain the following equation:

$$\tau \dot{P}_m + P_m = F'(P) \tag{7.11}$$

where $\tau = K_m/P_m$ and $F'(P) = F(P)/P_m$. This equation is of interest because of its simplicity and its utility in visualizing the process. That is, since this is the same type equation used to describe a RC low pass filter, we can draw an analogy between a pressure measurement and a simple filter. If we apply a step input to the pressure orifice, we expect the transducer to respond exponentially. Similarly, if we apply a sinusoidal input, we expect the transducer to respond with a similar waveform but perhaps attenuated in amplitude and shifted in phase.

Unlike the simple filter where the time constant is the product of resistance and capacitance, the time constant for the pressure measurement is an inverse function of the measured pressure. As the pressure decreases, the time constant increases. Consequently, the engineer should consider the extremes over which the measurement must operate when designing pneumatic systems. (**Note:** Measuring an oscillatory pressure may lead to a bias in the average value as a consequence of time constant variations.)

Other than the nature of the response, our primary interest is in the time constant. In its simplest form, the time constant, τ, can be expressed as:

$$\tau \simeq (l/d)(1/P) \tag{7.12}$$

Since l is normally fixed for a given application by transducer environmental and space considerations, it appears that tube diameter is the only free design parameter and the resulting problem is trivial. However, a single tube application such as presented here is rarely the case. More generally, a multitube configuration must be used, which requires using equivalent lengths and diameters to compute τ. Experimental determining τ for these applications is preferable.

7.3.1.2 Thermal Response

If a system whose temperature is T_1 is place in thermal contact with a system whose temperature is T_2, energy will be exchanged between the two systems until such time that thermal equilibrium is reached. This is the basic premise of classical non-optical temperature measurements that use thermocouples, thermistors, and resistance temperature detectors. The exchange of energy between the systems occurs as a result of heat transfer by conduction, radiation, and convection. Because of the various modes of heat transfer, thermal response is a more complex phenomenon to analyze than pneumatic response.

Consider the problem of quantifying the thermal response for a mass exposed to a moving fluid. Since the principal mode of heat transfer is forced convection, we can assume that heat transfer by both conduction and radiation is negligible. Based on this assumption, the system response can be described with the following equation:

$$\left(\frac{MC}{h_c A_c} \right) \dot{T}_m + T_m = T_E \tag{7.13}$$

where

M = the sensor mass in units of pounds

C = the sensor's specific heat in units of Btu/pound $\cdot$ °R

h_c = the coefficient of convection heat transfer in units of Btu/sec $\cdot$ ft^2 $\cdot$ °R

A_c = the heat transfer area in units of ft^2

T_m = the measured temperature in °R

T_E = the environment temperature in °R

At equilibrium, $\dot{T}_m$ is zero and the measured temperature T_m equals the environment temperature T_E. If the environment temperature is changed, the measured temperature tends to follow the change. There is, however, a lag as a result of the coefficient of the $\dot{T}_m$ term.

In the above equation, the coefficient of $\dot{T}_m$ is defined as the system time constant. Since the equation is a first-order linear differential equation, we expect the measurement to respond exponentially if T_E is subjected to a step change. After five time constants, the measured temperature will have reached 99.3 percent of the step change. Since the solution characteristics are well known for a linear first-order differential equation, it is not necessary to solve the equation. In fact, it is only necessary to determine the time constant using the following expression:

$$\text{Time Constant, } \tau = \frac{MC}{h_c A_c} \tag{7.14}$$

where the terms are as defined above and τ is in seconds.

7.3.2 Establishing Sampling Characteristics

The issue of sampling rate continues to mystify us. Misapplication of the Nyquist Sampling Theorem (interpreted by many as sample at twice the highest frequency where highest frequency is oftentimes mistakenly interpreted as the anti-alias filter's cutoff frequency) and incorrect interpretation of general rules of thumb, such as "sample at 5–10 times the highest frequency," are largely responsible for our confusion. Because of the criticality of sampling, it is essential that we establish sampling rate based on an analysis of our application's requirements and that we understand its implication on system specifications.

7.3.2.1 Sampling Rate vs. Filter Attenuation

In establishing sampling rate, we need to jointly consider both the ADC conversion rate and the anti-alias filter's characteristics in light of both the allowable distortion and the spectrum of the unfiltered phenomena to be measured.

As an example, assume that the function to be measured can be represented as shown in Figure 7.7a. Here, f_c denotes the highest frequency of interest even though there is energy extending all the way to $f_?$. If we use a filter with a cutoff frequency of f_c whose rolloff rate is R dB/octave, then we can conservatively establish the highest frequency as f_c^*. For this case, the sampler's output is shown in Figure 7.7b when a sampling frequency of $2f_c^*$ is used. Note that for this case, there is no distortion as evidenced by the spectrum being folded at f_c^*. Since we are only interested in frequencies up to f_c, we can permit distortion to occur between f_c and f_c^*. Here, we would choose the folding frequency, f_n, to be:

$$\log f_n = \log f_c + \frac{\log f_c^* - \log f_c}{2} = \tfrac{1}{2} (\log f_c + \log f_c^*) \tag{7.15}$$

If we are using a normalized f_c, then this reduces to:

$$f_n = \log^{-1} (\tfrac{1}{2} \log f_c^*) \tag{7.16}$$

This is shown in Figure 7.7c.

The graphical approach shown (Figure 7.7c) in choosing the folding frequency permits no distortion in the band of interest (i.e., from 0 to f_c). Here, the amplitude at which distortion can no longer be detected by the measurement system is defined as the ADC resolution. This is shown in Figure 7.7d. We can impose a more realistic distortion specification by permitting some distortion to occur in the band of interest. Thus, we might choose to specify that the maximum distortion at f_c is b dB (alternatively, we can state this as a percentage or that the alias must be attenuated by the amount b). With this criterion, we can reduce the sampling frequency to that shown in Figure 7.7e.

Once we have established an acceptable distortion level, we can use the following technique to compare sampling frequency for filters with different rolloff rates.

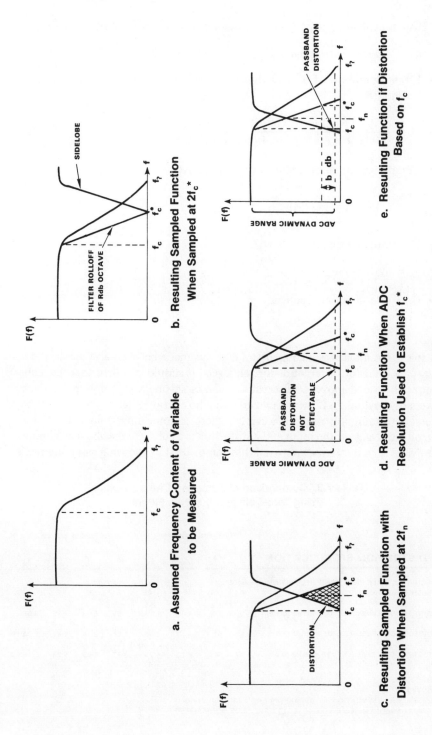

a. Assumed Frequency Content of Variable to be Measured

b. Resulting Sampled Function When Sampled at $2f_c^*$

c. Resulting Sampled Function with Distortion When Sampled at $2f_n$

d. Resulting Function When ADC Resolution Used to Establish f_c^*

e. Resulting Function if Distortion Based on f_c

Figure 7.7. Establishing Sampling Rate Based on Dynamic Distortion Considerations

- Compute distortion at f_c in dB based on specified percent of full scale

$$dB = 20 \log (\text{Percentage}) \tag{7.17}$$

- Establish number of octaves above f_c where input is attenuated by specified level in dB

$$N = \frac{\text{Attenuation in dB}}{\text{Filter Rolloff Rate in dB/octave}} \tag{7.18}$$

- Compute normalized frequency at this octave

$$\frac{f_c^*}{f_c} = \log^{-1}\left(N \log (2)\right) \tag{7.19}$$

- Determine folding frequency, f_n

$$f_n = \log^{-1} (\tfrac{1}{2} \log f_c^*) \tag{7.20}$$

- Compute sampling frequency, f_s

$$f_s \geq 2f_n \tag{7.21}$$

Table 7.3 summarizes a comparison that was made between a two-pole and a six-pole filter for different distortion levels. It should be noted that the technique illustrated above is conservative and is based on the assumption that there is energy beyond f_n. If there is evidence that no energy exists beyond f_n, we can relax the sampling rate. However, if there is some uncertainty about the frequency range of the input and if distortion is a concern, the above technique provides a conservative approach that can be used in choosing sampling rate.

Table 7.3. Comparison of Sampling Characteristics Using Two-Pole and Six-Pole Filters

DISTORTION SPECIFICATION	TWO-POLE FILTER				SIX-POLE FILTER			
	N	f_c^*	f_n	f_s	N	f_c^*	f_n	f_s
NO DETECTABLE PASS BAND DISTORTION WITH 12-BIT ADC (−72 dB)	6	64	8	16	2	4	2	4
DISTORTION LEVEL AT f_c OF −60 dB (0.1%)	5	32	5.66	11.3	1.67	3.18	1.78	3.56
DISTORTION LEVEL AT f_c OF −40 dB (1.0%)	3.33	10.1	3.18	6.36	1.11	2.16	1.47	2.94
DISTORTION LEVEL AT f_c OF −26 dB (5.0%)	2.17	4.5	2.12	4.24	0.72	1.65	1.28	2.56

NOTES:
1. FILTER ATTENUATION AT BREAKPOINT (f_c) ASSUMED ZERO
2. ALL FREQUENCIES LISTED (f_c^*, f_n, f_s) HAVE BEEN NORMALIZED BY f_c

7.3.2.2 Aperture and Sample/Hold Considerations

We can calculate the effects of aperture time on amplitude error based on an analysis of the amount an input sinusoidal at the highest frequency would change during a fixed aperture time. This can be used in conjunction with the ADC's resolution to quantify the effects of a given ADC's aperture on amplitude error or, alternatively, we can use ADC resolution and a budgeted aperture error to compute aperture time according to the equations listed in Chapter 6. If the error attributable to aperture time is excessive, we are required to implement a sample-and-hold circuit.

7.3.3 Implications of Bandwidth Considerations

An analysis of the bandwidth requirements will enable us to establish the following specifications on an individual measurement basis:

- ADC Conversion Rate
- ADC Aperture
- Sample-Hold Characteristics
- Anti-Alias Filter Characteristics
- System Bandwidth

As part of the overall performance analysis, we collectively consider these to establish aggregate throughput, multiplexer characteristics, and ADC-to-processor interface requirements.

7.4 PERFORMANCE

Traditionally, measurement and control functions have been separated. However, the marked improvements in processing hardware performance coupled with increased requirements for closed-loop control have promoted combining these functions. Since this significantly affects the functional design activity, we include these basic requirements in this chapter. It should be emphasized that this is a simplistic approach and is being included only to illustrate those global performance requirements we believe must be considered during functional design.

Generally speaking, the requirements that are applicable for most computer-based systems used for data acquisition and control and most significantly affect the functional design can be arranged in the following four categories:

1. **Measurements** — modes of data collection (e.g., burst, steady-state), data collection frequency and duration.

2. **Control** — type control, loop bandwidth

3. **Alarming** — number of parameters to be checked, frequency of checks, control strategies

4. **Displays** — number and type of displays, refresh time

Figure 7.8 is a simple data flow illustrating one way these four functions may be logically implemented. As shown, data in the form of counts are input at a rate determined by Clock A, converted to fundamental units, and then made available for all functions as either single sample or smoothed data (e.g., smoothing using either arithmetic averaging or digital filtering). These data are then commonly shared by other processing functions such as control, alarming, and display.

Figure 7.9 illustrates the relative timing for the critical control and alarming functions. Since data collection may involve sampling one or more inputs repetitively (burst mode) or collecting one sample for each input upon command, data collection is not shown as an event that occurs during each cycle. It should be noted that burst mode is in all likelihood the most stringent time performance specification. If the burst mode function is required in addition to control and alarming, the anticipated frequency of occurrence as well as burst duration must be considered since this degrades the overall performance. An analysis of burst characteristics in conjunction with critical control and alarming time requirements may suggest that this function be implemented with a separate processor.

To decompose the global performance requirements of control, alarming, and data collection into hardware performance specifications, it is instructive to look at the different times required to accomplish each step. For this, we need to have some prior knowledge of available hardware performance and to make some assumptions regarding the front end. Our approach is to estimate the times based on a chosen baseline configuration and to compare this to the requirement. Based on this comparison, there are two possibilities. First of all, the baseline's performance is such that the specification can be realized. For this case, there is no need to carry the analysis any further, provided that our system is not required to perform any additional tasks (i.e., the application is fixed). Secondly, the baseline's performance is such that the specification cannot be realized. For this case, the designer must alter the baseline system's performance. Options available are extensive and include using a processor that performs multiple tasks concurrently, using a faster processor or adding a hardware floating point processor, using a different analog-to-digital converter to processor interface, or using multiple converters and/or processors.

While the approach outlined above is simplistic, it does provide a methodology based on requirements for establishing processor characteristics (speed, interfaces, operating system, program language) and for determining the communications interface between the processor and critical peripheral devices. Since the performance characteristics are derived based on how the system is to

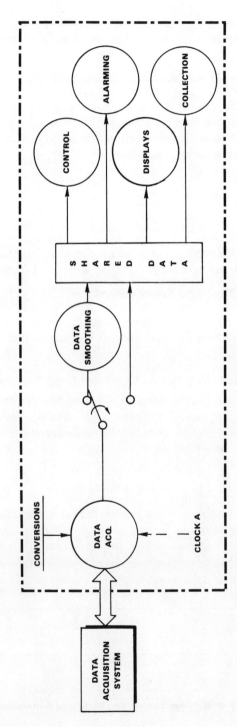

Figure 7.8. Data Flow For Control, Alarming, Display, and Data Collection Functions

be used (i.e., the context), they are only as good as our stated requirements. Thus, it is critical that the requirements that are based on context be comprehensive and accurate.

7.5 SYSTEM CONFIGURATION AND SPECIFICATIONS

As shown in Table 7.4, the above analyses enable us to specify on an individual parameter basis the performance requirements of both the sensor and the data system. We can finalize functional design by collectively considering the results of these analyses to determine the following:

- Data System Type
- Data System(s) Arrangement
- Processor Performance
- Configuration

Any miscellaneous requirements and/or constraints that were identified as part of the requirements are considered in finalizing equipment specifications.

7.5.1 Data System Type and Arrangement

When we collectively view the measurement and control requirements, we may elect to use more than one data system. The factors that influence this decision are:

- **Aggregate ADC Sampling Rate As Computed Using Bandwidth**

  Either the ADC's multiplexed sampling rate must be sufficient to satisfy all channels at the highest bandwidth or else different subsets must be digitized at different rates. Considerations include any software complexity attributa-

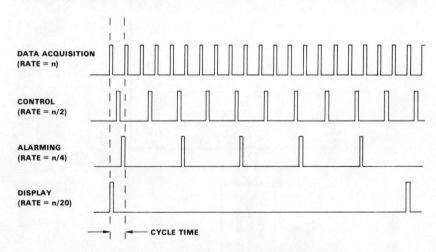

Figure 7.9. Relative Timing For Principal Functions

Table 7.4. Requirement Traceability

	REQUIREMENT	REMARKS
a. SENSOR		
• TYPE	ACCURACY	DETERMINE BASED ON ACHIEVABLE ACCURACY/RESPONSE PERFORMANCE
• RANGE	ACCURACY	DETERMINE BASED ON ACCURACY, REQUIRED RANGE, AND NUMBER
• NUMBER	ACCURACY	DETERMINE BASED ON SENSOR TURNDOWN AND ACCURACY EXTREMUMS
• ACCURACY	ACCURACY	ALLOCATE BASED ON TOTAL MEASUREMENT ACCURACY REQUIREMENT
• RESPONSE	BANDWIDTH	DETERMINE BASED ON TOTAL MEASUREMENT BANDWIDTH REQUIREMENT
• ENVIRONMENT	ACCURACY, OTHER	DETERMINE EFFECTS ON ACCURACY BASED ON ANTICIPATED ENVIRONMENT
b. POWER SUPPLY SPECS		
• CONSTANT V/CONSTANT I MODE	ACCURACY	COMPUTE $\frac{\partial e_o}{\partial R_L}\, \Delta R_L$
• RANGE	OTHER	DETERMINE IN CONJUNCTION WITH SENSOR
• LOCAL/REMOTE SENSE	OTHER	COMPUTE $\frac{\partial e_o}{\partial R_L}\, \Delta R_L + \frac{\partial e_o}{\partial V}\, \Delta V$
• CURRENT/VOLTAGE LIMITING	OTHER	DETERMINE IN CONJUNCTION WITH SENSOR
• LINE/LOAD REGULATION	ACCURACY	COMPUTE $\frac{\partial e_o}{\partial V}\, \Delta V$
• NOISE	ACCURACY	COMPUTE $\frac{\partial e_o}{\partial V}\, \Delta V$
• STABILITY	ACCURACY	COMPUTE $\frac{\partial e_o}{\partial V}\, \Delta V$
c. SIGNAL CONDITIONER (STRAIN GAGE)		
• BRIDGE COMPLETION	OTHER	DETERMINE IN CONJUNCTION WITH SENSOR
• OFFSET SUPPRESSION	ACCURACY	
— RESISTIVE BAL. VOLTAGE INSERT	ACCURACY	COMPARE SHUNTING LOAD ERROR TO VOLTAGE ERROR
— RANGE	OTHER	DETERMINE IN CONJUNCTION WITH SENSOR
— ACCURACY	ACCURACY	FOR RES BAL, DETERMINE SHUNT ERROR
• CALIBRATION		
— RESISTIVE CAL	OTHER	DETERMINE BASED ON MISCELLANEOUS REQUIREMENTS
— VOLTAGE INSERTION	OTHER	DETERMINE BASED ON MISCELLANEOUS REQUIREMENTS
d. SIGNAL CONDITIONER (THERMOCOUPLE)		
• REFERENCE JUNCTION TYPE	ACCURACY	CONSIDER REGULATION STABILITY VS READOUT ACCURACY
• REFERENCE ACCURACY	ACCURACY	COMPUTE ΔT
• CALIBRATION	OTHER	DETERMINE BASED ON MISCELLANEOUS REQUIREMENTS
e. AMPLIFIER		
• GAIN REQUIRED	ACCURACY/OTHER	DETERMINE IN CONJUNCTION WITH SENSOR OUTPUT
• ACCURACY	ACCURACY	
• INPUT IMPEDANCE	OTHER	DETERMINE IN CONJUNCTION WITH SENSOR IMPEDANCE
• CMRR	ACCURACY	DETERMINE BASED ON ERROR CONTRIBUTION AND CMV
• CMV MAX	OTHER	DETERMINE BASED ON MISCELLANEOUS REQUIREMENTS
• BANDWIDTH	BANDWIDTH	
• SLEW RATE	BANDWIDTH	
f. ANTI-ALIAS FILTER		
• TRANSFER ACCURACY	ACCURACY	
• ROLLOFF RATE	BANDWIDTH	DETERMINE IN CONJUNCTION WITH SAMPLING RATE
• PHASE NON-LINEARITY	BANDWIDTH	
• PASSBAND RIPPLE	ACCURACY	
g. ANALOG-TO-DIGITAL CONVERTER		
• TYPE (DUAL SLOP VS SUCCESSIVE APP.)	BANDWIDTH	DETERMINE BASED ON SAMPLING REQUIREMENT.
• RESOLUTION	ACCURACY	
• RANGE	ACCURACY	SELECT IN CONJUNCTION WITH SENSOR OUTPUTS AND SYSTEM GAIN
• TRANSFER ACCURACY	ACCURACY	
• CONVERSION RATE	BANDWIDTH	DETERMINE IN CONJUNCTION WITH FILTER ROLLOFF
• SAMPLE AND HOLD	BANDWIDTH	
• APERTURE	ACCURACY/ BANDWIDTH	
h. DIGITAL-TO-ANALOG CONVERTER		
• RESOLUTION	ACCURACY	
• VOLTAGE (CURRENT) OUT	OTHER	
• ISOLATION	OTHER	

ble to using different sampling rates with one ADC, the cost and complexity associated with using multiple data systems, each of which has a different data rate, and the penalty imposed on both the ADC-to-processor interface and software caused by multiple data systems.

• ADC-to-Processor Interface Based on ADC Sampling Rate

The performance characteristics of available interfaces must be sufficient to accommodate the aggregate data rate or multiple data systems must be used.

- **ADC Sampling Rate and Processor Interface Based on Global Requirements**

  The global performance requirements establish the cycle time, which in turn implies data rate.

- **Accuracy**

  If one common system is used, its accuracy must satisfy the most stringent requirement. If there is a wide variation in accuracy, there may be a cost advantage in using different systems. Considerations must be cost and any software complexity that results from this separation.

Regardless of whether we are using one or more data systems, there are some system characteristics that have not been addressed yet but must be considered. These are:

- **Data System Type**

  If the bandwidth analyses suggest using anti-alias filters whose rolloff is greater than 12 dB/octave or if there is a need to change filter cutoff frequency, the data system should be an amplifier-per-channel system that includes active filters.

- **Channel-to-Channel Phase**

  If data analysis will require using multiple channels (e.g., cross correlation), the channel-to-channel phase match must be specified.

- **Anti-Alias Filter**

  In specifying anti-alias filter characteristics, consideration must be given to nonlinear response and pass-band ripple as well as rolloff characteristics.

7.5.2 Configuration

There are a myriad of ways to put together hardware and software to form a system that will provide specific functions at quantifiable performance levels. Sometimes variations may exist because of the designer's experience or familiarity with similar systems or because of constraints such as hardware preference or other software requirements. Other times variations may exist simply as a result of how the designer chose to partition the problem.

In establishing the configuration, we suggest that the following approach be used:

- Clearly define all global functions (describe data acquisition methods, process control, control procedures, process monitoring).

- Describe interfaces to all other systems.

- Describe all outputs (reports, displays, graphics).

- Quantify performance requirements for each function using time and accuracy.

- Systematically decompose each function until an input/output boundary is reached.

- At each level of decomposition, establish the implications of the specified performance requirements.

We collectively consider all subfunctions, logically combine or group them as appropriate, and assign hardware/software to establish a configuration.

As an example, consider an application where the stated global function is to control and regulate the air velocity within a wind tunnel to a specified accuracy/time tolerance. This would be considered a primary function. We would through decomposition determine that the required subfunctions relate to measuring parameters such as pressure and temperature, computing variables, and outputting control signals. We use both global time and accuracy requirements to establish individual measurement accuracy, bandwidth, control updates, and output signal resolution. Since we are in all likelihood doing more than just controlling air velocity, we must determine how this function relates to other global functions such as controlling temperature and humidity, collecting data, and interfacing to the operator. We would collectively consider these to establish the configuration.

7.6 SUMMARY

We stated in Chapter 1 that our objectives were twofold. First, we wanted to develop a systematic design approach that would illustrate how a system could be designed based on general requirements. Second, we wanted to present analytical techniques that could be used to guide the system engineer in establishing a functional design and in developing detailed specifications. In doing both of these, we have concentrated on the fundamental design criteria of measurement accuracy and bandwidth. As we have seen, deciding how accurate a measurement must be made and how fast to sample are complex issues. However, these issues can be resolved systematically, thus providing a design approach framework.

It should be obvious that system design is a multifaceted task. While we can use analytical techniques to aid us in understanding the complex issues and in quantifying subsystem performance, there is no cookbook for this activity. The designer is confronted with numerous choices and tradeoffs. The analytical techniques simply make these visible for all to see.

References and Related Reading

In developing technical notes over the past several years, which eventually culminated with this manuscript, various references including texts, manufacturers' literature, and technical papers have been reviewed. It was this process of searching for a design guide that led me to conclude that simple application of the fundamentals of mathematics and engineering would produce a design in a systematic manner.

The references and related reading listed here pertain to the basics — measurement, sampling theory, and system components. The work by Abernethy establishes basic measurement uncertainty concepts and engineering methods for establishing these. The design problem from an accuracy viewpoint is simply the inverse of this. The collection of papers by Gordon and other equipment manufacturers' literature are excellent references. There are numerous texts on linear systems that are helpful in understanding sampling theory. Finally, the works of Benedict, Moffat, and Perino are excellent references for both the fundamentals and practical aspects of measurements.

1. Abernethy, R.B., et al. *Measurement Uncertainty Handbook*. Research Triangle Park: Instrument Society of America, 1980.

2. American Society for Testing and Materials. *Manual on the Use of Thermocouples in Temperature Measurement*. Philadelphia: ASTM, 1974.

3. Benedict, R.P. *Fundamentals of Temperature, Pressure, and Flow Measurements*. New York: John Wiley & Sons, 1984.

4. Breipohl, A.M. *Probabilistic Systems Analysis*. New York: John Wiley & Sons, Inc., 1970.

5. Chase, D. "Consider Every Error Source for Data Acquisition Design." *Control Engineering*, June 1980, pp. 65-69.

6. Cheng, D.K. *Analysis of Linear Systems*. Reading: Addison-Wesley Publishing Co., Inc., 1961.

7. Croxton, F.E., D.J. Cowden, and S. Klein. *Applied General Statistics*. Englewood Cliffs: Prentice-Hall, Inc., 1967.

8. Gordon, B.M., et al. *The Analogic Data-Conversion Systems Digest*. Wakefield: Analogic Corporation, 1977.

9. Hayt, W.H., and J.E. Kemmerly. *Engineering Circuit Analysis*. New York: McGraw-Hill, Inc., 1978.

10. Liptak, B.G. *Instrument Engineers' Handbook*, Vol. I & II. Philadelphia: Chilton Book Company, 1969.

11. Moffat, R.J. "Gas Temperature Measurement." *Measurement Engineering*, Vol. I. Phoenix: Stein Engineering Services, Inc., 1970.

12. Morrison, R. *Grounding and Shielding Techniques in Instrumentation.* New York: John Wiley & Sons, Inc., 1977.

13. Schwarz, R.J., and B. Friedland. *Linear Systems.* New York: McGraw-Hill, Inc., 1965.

14. Sheingold, D.H. *Analog-Digital Conversion Notes.* Norwood: Analog Devices, Inc., 1980.

15. Sheingold, D.H. *Transducer Interfacing Handbook.* Norwood: Analog Devices, Inc., 1980.

16. Perino, P.R. "Balance Networks for Whetstone Bridge Transducers." *Statham Instrument Notes.* Oxnard: Gould-Statham, Inc., 1967.

17. Perino, P.R. "System Considerations for Bridge Circuit Transducers." *Statham Instrument Notes.* Oxnard: Gould-Statham, Inc., 1964.

18. Perino, P.R. "Wheatstone Bridge Transducer Equations." *Statham Instrument Notes.* Oxnard: Gould-Statham, Inc., 1964.

19. Zuch, E.L. *Data Acquisition and Conversion Handbook, A Technical Guide to A/D and D/A Converters and Their Applications.* Mansfield: Datel-Intersil, 1980.

Appendix A

CASE STUDY: Functional Design of a High-Speed Computer-Based Data Acquisition System

A.1 INTRODUCTION

The effects of sudden impacts on both equipment and personnel are in some instances experimentally determined using facilities that accelerate a sled that is constrained to one-dimensional movement using a test track. The sled contains either equipment or mannequins that are instrumented to measure acceleration. The purpose of this case study is to present a technical approach that was used to design a high-speed computer-based data acquisition system.

A.2 REQUIREMENTS

The requirements listed below have been extracted from technical specifications prepared by others. For this case study, the specifications listed here were developed by a user organization and used to competitively procure a turnkey system for impact testing. Since the user developed the requirements in isolation, they are incomplete and are not representative of the requirements we advocated in the text. Unfortunately, this type of procurement where user organizations develop specifications internally and then solicit cost proposals from systems houses is typical. It is unfortunate in that the specifications are not generally the result of engineering analysis but rather are developed based on available equipment specifications. Extractions from the specifications are listed below as they were published. No attempt has been made to rewrite or to restate these.

Analog Input Channels — The system shall be capable of the collection and storage of 64 channels of analog data with a maximum voltage range of ± 10 V and the analysis bandwidths specified below. An input channel shall constitute a data path through the collection system starting at the output of a signal transducer and terminating in data storage within the system.

Analog Output Channels — The system shall be capable of the parallel transmission of 8 channels of analog data reconstructed from the digital data stored in the system memory. All analog output signals shall be capable of a maximum voltage range of ± 10 V dc, and shall be capable of driving a 10 kΩ load at the maximum output voltage. All analog output signals shall be available in the single-ended output mode. The system shall be capable of the simultaneous outputting of 8 channels of analog data whose individual bandwidths are dc to 5 kHz. An output channel shall constitute a data path starting in system memory and terminating as a reconstructed analog signal.

Accuracy — The mean squared error between a system analog input and a reconstructed analog output shall not exceed 0.2% of the mean squared value of the system output. That is:

$$\frac{\displaystyle\int_{T_1}^{T_2} [y(t) - x(t)]^2 \, dt}{\displaystyle\int_{T_1}^{T_2} [y(t)]^2 \, dt} \times 100 \leq 0.2 \text{ for } T_1 < t < T_2$$

where

$x(T)$ = the analog input signal voltage
$y(T)$ = the analog output signal voltage
$T_2 - T_1$ = the analysis interval

subject to the following conditions:

- All input signals are considered to be of the low pass type.

- The output signal shall be reconstructed from the digitally stored data.

- The stated accuracy shall apply individually to each input/output channel pair with the system operating at a data rate up to the maximum rate for all channels.

- The stated accuracy applies only for signals within the analysis bandwidth under consideration.

- For the exclusive purpose of making this measurement, the input signal can be a sine wave. System gain is assumed to be unity.

This system accuracy must be met under actual test conditions, i.e., equipment mounted on the sled undergoing acceleration and signals being transmitted through the data cable to the instrumentation room.

Analog Data Sampling Frequency — The sampling frequency (F_s) shall be high enough to permit an accurate reproduction of signals in any one analog input channel in the analysis bandwidth as specified below. (F_s) shall be selectable manually or under computer control and is dependent on the highest frequency of interest in the analysis bandwidth, the attenuation slope or rolloff of the anti-aliasing filter, and the maximum level of attenuation desired to the aliasing frequencies. The highest frequency in the analysis band shall not be attenuated by more than 0.1 dB and all aliases shall be attenuated by at least 80 dB. The system shall be capable of a maximum sampling rate, which will permit the simultaneous collection of 64 channels of analog data with a bandwidth from dc to 5 kHz.

Anti-Aliasing Filters — Each analog input channel shall be provided with an anti-aliasing filter. The cutoff frequency of each filter shall be independently selectable both under computer and manual control for the analysis bandwidth desired. Each filter shall provide a computer or manually controlled fixed gain of 1, 2 and 5 as a minimum requirement. Pass-band ripple shall be 0.1 dB or less.

Single Channel Phase Response — The maximum deviation of the phase response from a linear phase response for any individual channel shall not exceed $\pm 2.5°$ within the analysis bandwidth.

Channel-to-Channel Phase Matching — The phase characteristics of any two input or any two output channels must not deviate from one another by more than $\pm 1°$ within the analysis bandwidth.

Minimum and Maximum Analysis Times — The system shall be capable of collecting and storing 64 channels of analog data for time intervals from a minimum of 10 milliseconds to a maximum of 1 second at the maximum sampling rate. Time intervals between the minimum and maximum analysis times shall be continuously selectable with an accuracy of ± 25 microseconds.

Analysis Bandwidth — The data bandwidth of any input or output channel shall be operator selectable from a minimum of dc to 2.5 Hz to a maximum of dc to 25 kHz subject to sampling frequency restrictions.

System Calibration Program — A program shall be provided that will verify that the Data Acquisition System is operating within the system performance requirements. The program shall identify which elements of the system are not functioning and should calibrate or aid in the system calibration so that operation is again within the system specification.

Data Collection Program — A program shall be provided that will sense the start of a test and record automatically up to 64 channels of analog data into the data memory. The program shall enable the operator to set the number of input data channels and select the analysis bandwidth, data collection interval, sampling rate and gain of each input channel signal conditioner. The program shall enable the operator to review any channel of collected data after the test and to output the data in graphic and tabular form on the operator console and hard copy devices.

Transducer Calibration Program — A program shall be supplied that shall input synthetic or test dc voltages into any input channel for the purpose of calibrating the test transducers. Provisions shall be included to store transducer calibration data on the mass storage devices and to output this data on the hard copy devices.

Temperature — The system shall be capable of operation at a temperature of $20° \pm 10°C$. Any equipment installed on the test sled shall be capable of operating at a temperature of $20° \pm 20°C$. The system shall be capable of surviving temperatures from $-10°C$ to $70°C$ in a nonoperating condition without damage.

Humidity - Components of the data acquisition system located in the instrumentation room shall be capable of operation at a relative humidity from 0% to 90%. Components located on the test sled, including the data cable, shall be capable of operation from 0% to 100% relative humidity, including condensation.

Shock — Any electronic components located on the test sled shall be capable of operation with the specified performance during repeated shock loadings of 100 g's trapezoidal pulse of 90 msec duration with an onset rate of 1500 g/sec. The data cable and cable attachment hardware shall be capable of surviving repeated shock loadings of 70 g's trapezoidal pulse 90 msec duration with an identical onset rate.

Vibration — Components located on the test sled shall be capable of operation within the specified performance requirements during exposure to sinusoidal vibrations of 0.6 inch double amplitude at frequencies from 5 to 60 Hz, and of 35 g's RMS from 60 Hz to 2 kHz.

NOTE: For this application, the supplier had the option of putting some equipment on the test sled. In considering the environmental constraints listed above, this option was considered to be a high risk item and thus inappropriate for a fixed price contract. Accordingly, a decision was made to propose a system design where all equipment was located in the control room that is approximately 200 feet from the sled.

A.3 ANALYSIS

A.3.1 Static Accuracy

If we evaluate the specified accuracy integral at zero frequency, we obtain the following:

$$\frac{\displaystyle\int_{T_1}^{T_2} [y(t) - x(t)]^2 dt}{\displaystyle\int_{T_1}^{T_2} [y(t)]^2 dt} \leq \frac{0.2}{100}$$

Let

$$E = y(t) - x(t)$$

and

$$y(t) = C$$

Then,

$$\frac{\displaystyle\int_{T_1}^{T_2} E^2 dt}{\displaystyle\int_{T_1}^{T_2} C^2 dt} \leq 0.002$$

$$\frac{E^2(T_2 - T_1)}{C^2(T_2 - T_1)} \leq 0.002$$

$$E \leq [(0.002)C^2]^{\frac{1}{2}}$$

$$E \leq (0.044)C$$

Thus, the static accuracy requirement is interpreted to be 0.044 × input. If we use a data system with a measurement uncertainty of 0.2% F.S., then the minimum input level that can be measured and be within specifications is:

$$0.044C = 0.2\% \text{ F.S.}$$

For F.S. = 10 V, $C = 0.45$ V. Measurements made with a 0.2% F.S. data system at voltages less than this will be in error outside specifications.

A.3.2 Dynamic Accuracy

There are several areas of concern for dynamic signals. These are discussed below.

1. Filter Pass-band Ripple

The specifications list an acceptable pass-band ripple of 0.1 dB. For full scale inputs (± 10 V), this ripple specification corresponds to an error of:

$$0.1 \text{ dB} = 20 \log \left(\frac{e_o}{e_1} \right), \ e_1 = 10 \text{ V}$$

$$e_o = 9.885$$

The error is

$$\text{Error} = \left(\frac{e_1 - e_o}{e_1} \right) \times 100 = 1.2\%$$

At an input level of 1 V, the ripple component constitutes an error of 11.4% of reading.

2. Aperture Consideration

An approximation to the converter's required aperture time can be made by assuming a sinusoidal input and establishing the time required such that the input changes less than the resolution. For a 14-bit converter with a 5 kHz input, the computed time to maintain error less than resolution is 3.9 nsec.

- Amplitude Error, % $= (1 - \sin x / x) \, 100$

    where $x = \pi \Delta T f$

- Phase Lag, Degrees $= \pi \Delta T f$

3. Input Filter Considerations

The cable connecting the test sled transducer to the conditioning equipment has both capacitance and resistance associated with it. Since the line resistance is negligible compared to the transducer's output impedance, it can be ignored. The cable capacitance in conjunction with the transducer impedance forms a low pass RC filter that acts to attenuate high frequencies. By lumping all cable capacitance and using typical cable specifications of 50 picofarad/foot (C) and output sensor impedances of 300 ohms (R), the effective filter for a 200-foot cable can be computed as follows:

$$RC = (300) (50 \times 10^{-12} \text{ f/foot}) (200 \text{ feet})$$

$$RC = 3 \times 10^{-6} \text{ seconds}$$

The filter's transfer function is:

$$G(j\omega) = \frac{1}{1 + j\omega RC}$$

The errors attributable to input cabling are defined by the following:

- Amplitude $|G(j\omega)| = \dfrac{1}{(1 + (\omega RC)^2)^{\frac{1}{2}}}$

- Phase $\theta = -\tan^{-1}(\omega RC)$

Hence, the effective filter for the cable and sensor has a cutoff frequency of 53 kHz.

In accordance with the specification, it is desired to process information for all sensors at frequencies up to 5 kHz and for limited channels up to 25 kHz. The errors introduced at these frequencies as a result of the cabling are computed to be:

Errors at 5 kHz

- Amplitude: 0.44 percent
- Phase: −5.4°

Errors at 25 kHz

- Amplitude: 9.5 percent
- Phase: −25°

4. Reconstruction Error

The sampled data are to be used to reconstruct the continuous signal using a digital-to-analog converter and then this analog output is to be compared to the input to quantify error. The error resulting from using a finite set of digital data to represent a continuum are described by a zero-order hold. They are:

- Amplitude Error, $\% = (1 - \sin x / x)\,100$

  where $x = \pi(f/fs)$

- Phase Lag, Degrees $= \pi(f/fs)$

This error can be reduced using interpolating techniques and/or an analog smoothing filter.

5. ADC Resolution

Based on the magnitude of the errors shown above, it would be difficult to justify using a converter where resolution is greater than, say, 12 bits. However, the requirement that all aliases be attenuated by at least 80 dB implies that the system's dynamic range is at least 80 dB. Thus,

Dynamic Range, dB $= 20 \log$ (ADC Resolution)

Resolution $= 0.0001$

Thus, a 14-bit ADC including sign is required to provide 80 dB dynamic range.

A.3.3 Bandwidth

1. Determining Sampling Rate, fs

The specified bandwidth is 5 kHz expandable to 25 kHz for selected channels with all aliases attenuated by at least 80 dB. Table A.1 summarizes filter/sampling considerations based on an 80 dB distortion specification. Equations 7.17 – 7.21 and Equation 6.16 are applicable.

Table A.1. Filtering & Sampling Rate Considerations

Rolloff Rate	N	f_c	fn	fs
12 dB/octave	$6.\overline{6}$	500.0 kHz	50.0 kHz	100.0 kHz
24	$3.\overline{3}$	50.0	15.8	31.6
36	$2.\overline{2}$	23.2	10.8	21.5
48	$1.\overline{6}$	15.8	8.9	17.8
80	1	10.0	7.1	14.1

Based on these data, the individual channel sampling rate required for a 5 kHz bandwidth varies from approximately 14 kHz to 100 kHz depending upon the filter's rolloff rate.

In establishing the sampling considerations in Table A.1, it was assumed that the filter's cutoff frequency, f_c, was positioned exactly at 5 kHz. No consideration was given to the actual rolloff characteristics within the passband or to the phase specification. The specifications, however, require that the attenuation at 5 kHz be less than 0.1 dB. Additionally, phase linearity must be within ± 2.5°. Depending upon the filter selected, these criteria may require that the filter's cutoff be positioned at a frequency greater than f_c. If so, this will affect the above data. Accordingly, the next logical step is to select a filter and then recompute the required sampling rate.

2. Finalizing Filter Selection

In selecting a filter, our primary concerns are phase linearity, amplitude, overshoot, and ringing. The phase linearity and transient response characteristics of both the Chebyshev and Butterworth are such that both filters can be immediately discounted. While the phase and transient response characteristics of the Bessel filter are acceptable, the amplitude characteristics within the pass-band require repositioning of the cutoff frequency to meet specifications and thus impose a significant penality on sampling frequency. Based on these considerations and on other specified filter attributes (remotely programmable cutoff frequency, channel-to-channel phase match, and different fixed gains), the decision was made to use an elliptic filter. However, even with the elliptic filter, repositioning of the cutoff frequency is necessary to achieve phase linearity within the desired passband.

The characteristics of the selected elliptic filter are:

- Rolloff Rate: 80 dB/octave

- Ripple: 0.1 dB pass-band and stop-band

- Phase Linearity: Linear over the range

$$0.1 \leq \frac{f}{fc} \leq 0.33$$

3. Finalizing Sampling Frequency

For a desired bandwidth of 5 kHz, we reposition the filter's cutoff to 15 kHz to achieve linear phase. Using f_c = 15 kHz, we compute the following:

- Number of octaves, N = 1

- Effective Cutoff Frequency, f_c^* = 30 kHz

- Folding Frequency, f_n = 21.2 kHz
- Sampling Frequency, f_s = 42.4 kHz

It should be noted that for f_s = 42.4 kHz, the amplitude attenuation for the true frequency range of interest (i.e., f_c = 5 kHz) caused by the first-order hold characteristics of the DAC is:

- Amplitude Error, % = $(1 - \sin x / x)\,100$

  = 2.3%

- Phase Lag, Degrees = $\pi\,(f/f_s)$

  = 3.7°

A.4 FUNCTIONAL DESIGN

A.4.1 Signal Conditioning/Amplifier

Although not included in the requirements stated above, the user's specifications described the signal conditioning requirements in detail. To accommodate both strain gage and piezoresistive sensors, signal conditioning that provides both excitation and offset adjustment as well as accommodates shunt calibrations is required. The user's specification described automatic bridge balancing and automatic shunt calibration features also.

Each channel was required to include a differential amplifier with stated performance characteristics such as a CMRR of 80 dB, a differential input impedance of 20 megohms, offset current of 30 nA, adjustable sensitivity from ± 1 to ± 1,000 mV, maximum CMV of ± 5 V dc, and be capable of withstanding overvoltages of ± 250 V dc.

It should be noted that most of the specific criteria listed in the user's requirements are inappropriate. These details should be the consequence of the designer's analysis and thus established based on accuracy, bandwidth, and other miscellaneous requirements. If the user specifies overall performance requirements such as accuracy and bandwidth, it is inappropriate to state subsystem performance characteristics such as sensor power supply character-istics (these are determined based on sensor error analysis), amplifier charac-teristics such as CMRR (this is based on an error analysis), amplifier offset current, and input impedance. It should be noted that the user's requirements did not address amplifier slew rate or bandwidth — both of which are important for this type of transient testing. However, they are also inappropriate if included in the user's requirements.

A.4.2 Multiplexer/ADC

The bandwidth analysis presented earlier is based on individual channel requirements. However, the system is required to support 32 channels concurrently. (Note: The user's requirement of 64 channels was reduced to state 32 channels expandable to 64 channels.) From an implementation point of view, it is preferable if a multiplexer/ADC is chosen that has the sampling capability to accommodate all 32 channels. If this is not possible, we will be required to use multiple front ends, which complicates both hardware and software. We establish an aggregate throughput, F_s, based on the sampling frequency, f_s, required for 5 kHz bandwidth as follows.

$$F_s = \text{(No. Channels)} \, (f_s)$$

$$F_s = 1{,}357 \text{ kHz}$$

At the time of this equipment selection, there were only a limited number of 14-bit multiplexed ADC's on the marketplace that were considered acceptable. The unit chosen for additional consideration was rated at 1 MHz, 15-bit, aperture time of 1 nsec, and could support 32 channels. Based on this, two separate ADC's are required to achieve an effective aggregate throughput of 1.357 MHz.

Using two separate 1 MHz ADC's, the processor must be capable of accepting two 2 Mbyte/second data streams concurrently. The processor's I/O bandwidth must thus be 4 Mbyte/second.

NOTE: When this issue was discussed with the user, he decreased his individual channel bandwidth requirement from 5 kHz to 2 kHz. This had the effect of reducing the individual channel sampling rate from 42.4 kHz to 17 kHz. The aggregate bandwidth, F_s, is thus 544 kHz. This enables all 32 channels to be processed using one 1 MHz ADC.

A.4.3 Configuration

Although there are several large computer vendors with acceptable products, we chose to use Hewlett Packard® (HP) for the base-line. The distributed architecture of the new HP1000 Series A™ processor provides for increased I/O efficiency by incorporating individual I/O processors on each interface card. The system is supported by a multiprogramming, multiuser, real-time executive operating system and is capable of executing 10^6 instructions per second.

In establishing the computer system requirements, prime consideration was given to the I/O bandwidth. As noted before, there are two-2 Mbyte/sec data streams that must be accepted by the computer system when all 64 channels are operating at the maximum sampling rate. This translates to an effective I/O bandwidth of 4 Mbyte/second.

As shown in Figure A.1, we elected to use a distributed processing network consisting of a host and two node processors. This degree of complexity is a direct consequence of the high I/O requirement. The preprocessors are interfaced directly to the converters and provide capability for the high throughput by placing data directly into preprocessor memory. At these transmission rates, it is not practical to place data in disc memory. Consequently, each preprocessor is equipped with 4 Mbyte main memory, which is adequate to cover the maximum run time of one second.

The preprocessors are linked to a host processor by distributed system hardware/software. Upon completion of a test, data are routed from each preprocessor to the host, where it is placed on disc and/or magnetic tape. The host processor is equipped with various peripherals such as a disc, 9-track magnetic tape unit, 8-pin plotter, line printer, graphics terminal, and a system console terminal.

A.5 SUMMARY

As can be seen from this example, there are numerous technical issues associated with establishing a functional system design. It is possible to use simple engineering techniques to aid the systems engineer in logically developing the concept and in selecting equipment. More importantly, this approach provides assurance that, once the system is built, the overall performance will not be a surprise to either the designer or user. Additional information regarding this example can be found in a paper by James W. Hayes and Laura J. Hart entitled "Acquiring Dynamic Data from Impact Testing Using a Sampled Data System," *Instrumentation In The Aerospace Industry, Volume 31*, Proceedings of the 31st International Instrumentation Symposium, San Diego, California, May 6–9, 1985.

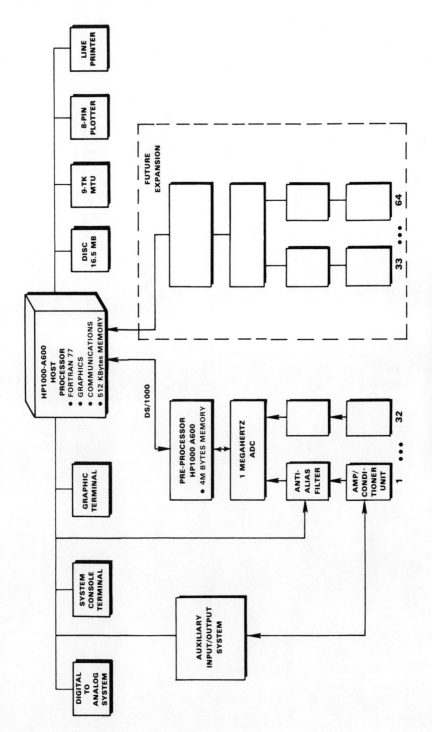

Figure A.1. System Block Diagram

Appendix B

CASE STUDY: Functional Design of a Multichannel Computer-Based Data Acquisition and Control System for Climatic Test Facilities

B.1 INTRODUCTION

Since automobile manufacturers are concerned with all aspects of passenger vehicles including those that affect human comfort, considerable emphasis is placed on all aspects of a vehicle's heating and cooling system. Tests are conducted both on the road as well as in environmentally controlled test facilities to evaluate the integrated performance of a vehicle's heating and cooling system. Because of the relatively long development times associated with new vehicles, testing programs for a specific prototype may last for several years. All during this development cycle, changes are made to the baseline system, and tests are conducted to quantify the effects of a change. Thus, it becomes critical that the accuracy of data obtained over a long time period and from both road tests and test facilities be comparable.

The purpose of this case study is to present some of the more important issues as they relate to the material presented in the text for the case where we are to design a computer-based data acquisition and control system for a climatic test facility. Because of the complexity of the design problem, only a few key issues are addressed.

B.2 REQUIREMENTS

The test facility is a closed-loop environmental wind tunnel sized to accommodate full size passenger vehicles and light trucks. Typical capabilities include simulating vehicle speeds of 120 mph (this requires both wind tunnel air speed and chassis rolls dynamometer speed), establishing temperatures ranging from $-25°$ F to $+125°$ F at relative humidities ranging from 20–90%, and simulating solar loads. A summary of requirements is listed below.

B.2.1 Measurements

Test Vehicle

Vehicle measurement requirements vary as a function of test objectives. To accommodate a variety of tests, the system shall be configured as a general purpose measurement system equipped with a disconnect panel located in the test cell. Specific input requirements are listed below.

- Types of phenomena: pressure, temperature, voltages, currents, flows, and speeds
- Temperature accuracies: $\pm 0.2°$ F to $\pm 4°$ F
- Pressure accuracies: $\pm 0.1\%$ FS to 1.0% FS
- Voltages and Currents: $\pm 0.5\%$ FS

Facility

Specific measurement requirements include all probes, sensors, signal conditioning, and wiring necessary to measure the primary parameters (air speed, temperature, relative humidity) and secondary parameters (solar load, solar load position, fan speed, and brine flow). Specific requirements for each measurement are listed below.

- Air speed accuracy: $\pm 0.5\%$ reading
- Temperature: $\pm 0.5°$ F
- Barometric pressure: $\pm 0.1\%$ reading
- Relative humidity: $\pm 0.5\%$

B.2.2 Controls

Test Vehicle

- Remotely control throttle to regulate either vehicle speed or establish torque, depending upon the dynamometer's regulation mode.
- Remotely control up to three different vehicle voltages.

Facility

- Control airspeed by varying wind tunnel's fan speed. An existing closed-loop fan speed controller is to be integrated within new system.
- Control temperature by varying flow rate through existing heat exchanger.
- Control humidity by mixing outside air and/or by injecting either steam or water.
- Control chassis rolls dynamometer. The existing dynamometer operates in either speed or torque regulation modes and is to be integrated with the new

system such that the system can remotely change regulation modes and can supply set points.

- Remotely turn on/off one or more of seven different light banks.

B.2.3 Other Requirements

Operation Philosophy

To accommodate both standard and developmental testing, the system design shall support three test cell modes of operation — automatic, semi-automatic, and manual. The automatic mode shall be designed to support those tests that can be well defined in advance. For this mode, the test engineer shall specify the complete sequence prior to testing. This shall include specifying cell conditions, vehicle conditions, simulated road conditions, timing, and data collection.

The mechanism used to convey this information to the system shall be a Test Matrix. The test matrix shall consist of as many as 50 distinct entries, where each entry is used to describe a unique set of steady-state test conditions. Each entry also contains cell and vehicle transitional parameters that describe the trajectories to be used in advancing from the present conditions to the next set of conditions.

Using an input terminal device, the operator initiates testing by identifying the desired test matrix. Following a series of predefined operational checks, the first set of conditions are established. During this time, all data inputs are continuously monitored, compared to upper and lower limits, and displayed. In the event that any critical parameters are out of limits, any of several strategies are executed in accordance with the alarming severity. Strategies may include executing either an implied pause or shutting the tunnel down.

Once it has been determined that either the data are stabilized or a maximum time has been expended at this condition, data are captured and stored. If there are remaining test conditions, the matrix specified transitional parameters (e.g., ramp, rate-of-change, etc.) are used by the control algorithms to move from one steady-state condition to another and thus establish new conditions. The process of establishing conditions and collecting data continues until either all specified conditions in the test matrix have been obtained or the test cell operator aborts the test.

Miscellaneous

The system shall be designed to accommodate general-purpose testing. This requires that the measurement system be capable of accommodating a wide range of analog and discrete inputs and that the acquisition program be easily configurable by nonprogramming personnel.

The system shall provide real-time data acquisition and display within each cell. All analog parameters shall be converted into either metric units (e.g., Pascal, newton-meter, ° C, etc.) or English units for display. The choice shall be operator selectable. Conversion constants shall be easily changeable by the cell operator and shall not require software code modifications.

The system design shall provide archival data storage and data base management capabilities. During testing, the system shall provide the capability to compare, in an on-line mode, current test results with previous stored test results. Upon completion of a test in any cell, the system shall provide centralized permanent data storage. For data security, various levels of passwords shall be implemented.

B.3 ANALYSIS

B.3.1 Accuracy

As we alluded to in the introductory section, the fact that tests are conducted over a relatively long time both within different test facilities and on the road requires that we be concerned with absolute measurement uncertainty as well as precision errors. Of the different measurements required for the tunnel, it is necessary that the measurements used to define an operating condition (air velocity, temperature, and relative humidity) be precise and unbiased. This is fundamental if comparisons of any vehicle measurements are to be successful. Each of the primary measurements is discussed below.

1. Air Velocity

Air Velocity, V, is computed using Bernoulli's equation for noncompressible fluids.

$$V = [2q/\rho]^{1/2}$$

where

V = velocity, m/sec
q = dynamic pressure, Pascals
ρ = air density, kg/m^3

Air density is computed using the following equation:

$$\rho = P/RT$$

where

P = total pressure, Pascals
R = gas constant for air, 287.1 J/kg/°K
T = total temperature, °K

The climatic cell is an atmospheric pressure tunnel designed to operate over a velocity range of 0–120 mph (0–193 km/Hr) at temperatures ranging from –25°F to +125°F (241–325°K). Figure B.1 illustrates computed dynamic pressure as a function of air velocity for the two different temperature extremes.

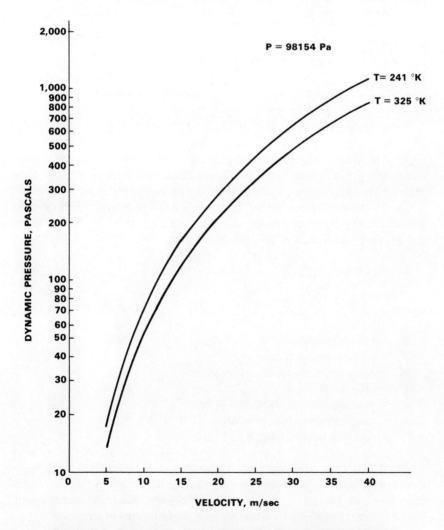

Figure B.1. Dynamic Pressure Range For Temperature Extremes

We expand the velocity equation in a Taylor series, apply the RSS, evaluate the partials at the desired operating velocity extremes (3.93 and 39.3 m/s) and temperature extremes (241 and 325° K), and solve for the individual maximum allowable errors in the three measurement. This is the same technique illustrated in Example 3.3. The results of these calculations are summarized in Table B.1. The errors listed in Table B.1 represented the maximum total measurement error. We use these as design criteria as described below.

**Table B.1. Measurement Error Guidelines
Based on 0.5% Velocity Error Considerations**

Measurement	Range	Total Error
Dynamic Pressure	0–1200 Pa	<1.0% Reading
Total Temperature	−32°C to +52°C	<2.5°C
Total Pressure	0.9–1.0 Bar	<0.5% Reading

2. Total Temperature

Total airstream temperature is a critical parameter used in evaluating climatic conditioning equipment. Since the fluid stream whose temperature is to be measured has kinetic energy, the temperature measurement of the moving fluid will be less than total temperature. This error is a function of air velocity and the recovery factor of the temperature probe. The error attributable to air velocity can be computed using the following equations:

Velocity Error $= T_A - T_J = (1-\alpha) V^2/(2gJCp)$

where

T_A = total temperature, °R
T_J = probe junction temperature, °R
α = probe recovery factor, dimensionless
V = velocity, ft/sec
g = gravitational constant, 32.174 ft/sec^2
J = mechanical equivalent of heat, 778 ft-lb/Btu
Cp = specified heat of fluid, 0.24 Btu/lb°R

Figure B.2 illustrates the temperature measurement error attributable to velocity for the climatic cell's velocity range. For these data, a probe recovery factor of 0.7 was used. This error, which represents a negative bias in the measurement, can be reduced by using a total temperature probe located in an area of low air velocity.

Because of the criticality of this measurement, it is recommended that multiple measurements be made and mathematically combined to establish average total temperature. Four to six probes placed around the internal shell and averaged will compensate for any temperature stratification and thus provide an accurate measure of the average airpath temperature at the vehicle interface. To reduce the effects of air velocity, the total temperature probes are to be located in a low velocity region between the fan exit and the nozzle entrance.

Because of the relatively large bias errors associated with thermocouples (using a Type T thermocouple, the error over the range of interest with the thermocouple is $\pm 1.5°$F, which must be combined with other measurement system errors), it is recommended that platinum resistive temperature detectors rather than thermocouples be used. With proper precautions, this technique will provide an absolute accuracy better than $0.5°$F. This more than satisfies the temperature accuracy requirement dictated by the velocity error criterion.

NOTES:

a. At this point, we need to be cautious. While an RTD is appropriate, the cabling connecting the RTD to the data system will be exposed to temperatures ranging from $-25°$F to $+125°$F. If we are using a three-wire configuration, this produces a significant bias error. We can use the equations and methods described in Example 5.2 to compute the change in line resistance that will result for a specific installation. We would be remiss if at this point we did not acknowledge that there are other ways of connecting a three-wire RTD other than the way we have chosen, which does not introduce as large an error. Our purpose in avoiding this has been to create an awareness that attention must be paid to sensor/equipment interface details.

b. Statistical techniques such as the Thompson Tau Method are preferred for mathematically combining the different temperatures. By computing a standard deviation and then comparing each individual measurement to the average combined with a multiple of this deviation, suspect measurements can be discarded.

---

3. Relative Humidity

To achieve the desired accuracy in the RH measurement, it is necessary to use a measurement technique such as the optical hygrometer, which operates on the chilled mirror dew-point principal. This technique, however, requires a sampling system and thus leakage, pressure, and temperature gradients as well as moisture absorption/desorption characteristics must be considered. Addi-

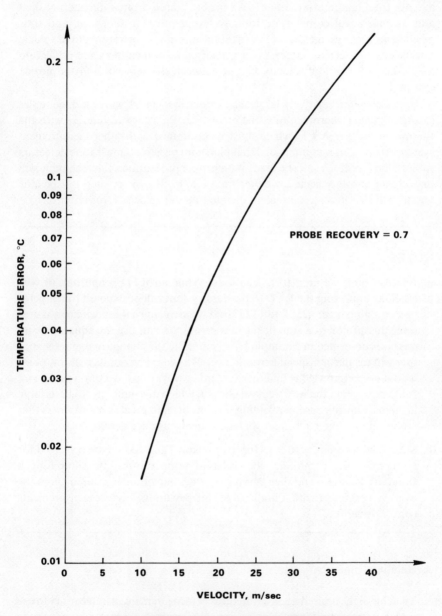

**Figure B.2. Error in Temperature Measurement
Resulting From Non-Zero Velocity**

tionally, the mirror is subject to contamination, which affects mirror reflectance. If the sensor associated with RH is located within the tunnel, all of the comments regarding error with RTDs are applicable here. If the instrument does not use a 4-wire measurement technique, large bias errors are possible, thus compromising the measurement.

4. Dynamic Pressure

The sensor must provide measurements accurate to ± 1% of reading over the range of 10–1,000 Pa. This translates to providing a measurement whose overall accuracy is ±0.01% FS. A review of Table 7.2 suggests that a capacitance manometers with a sensor uncertainty of ±0.08% of reading is more than adequate. Note that to avoid compromising the sensor's accuracy a manometer with internal signal conditioning and conversion is required.

5. Other Measurements

Since this is to be a general-purpose measurement system, there are no other standard performance parameters we can use to establish individual measurement accuracy requirements. Discussions with the user indicated the need for absolute accuracy with several of the temperature measurements. This was interpreted as a requirement for RTD's. Here, again, a four-wire configuration is required. Similar discussions regarding pressure measurements indicated stringent accuracy requirements for several of the low pressure differential measurements. This was interpreted to mean capacitance manometers.

B.3.2 Bandwidth

Climatic testing is essentially steady-state testing. That is, a set of conditions (air speed, temperature, RH, load) is established, the vehicle is allowed to stabilize (achieve equilibrium with cell environment), and data are collected. For this testing mode, one sample for each channel would be sufficient to define the experiment, assuming that there were no fluctuations. However, in practice there are small variations in a measurement resulting from either fluctuations in the phenomenon to be measured or electrical noise. For steady state, these variations are unwanted and must be averaged such that the captured value represents the measured average. Thus, a filtering scheme must be employed.

Although climatic testing is basically steady state, there is a need for transient testing. This is a consequence of the compressor cycling on and off during certain air conditioning tests, which causes cyclic variations in certain pressure and temperature parameters. For each of these parameters, an adequate number of samples is required to quantify the cyclic variations such as minimum and maximum values and cycle duration time.

An estimate of sampling rate can be established by assuming that the phenomenon to be measured is sinusoidal (because of the cyclic nature, this is believed to be a reasonable assumption). For this case, the input can be represented as:

$$F = A \sin(\omega t)$$

where A is amplitude and ω is angular frequency. At a point, the incremental change in F, δF, can be computed as follows:

$$\delta F = F' \Delta T$$

where

$$F' = A\omega \cos(\omega t)$$

Using these relationships, an expression for ΔT in terms of a specified change in $F (\delta F)$ at an angular frequency ω is:

$$\Delta T = \delta F / A\omega \cos(\omega t)$$

Since the cosine function has amplitude limits of ± 1, this reduces to

$$\Delta T = \delta F / A\omega$$

Specifying δF as a percentage of amplitude yields

$$\Delta T = (AX100)/A\omega = (X100)/\omega$$

where X is the specified percentage of reading error.

If samples are acquired at this ΔT rate, then the maximum error for sinusoidals is equal to or less than the specified amplitude percentage error. Figure B.3 illustrates the relationship of individual channel sampling rate as a function of compressor cycling rate for 0.5 and 1.0 percent of reading error. Although the phenomenon is relatively low frequency, a high sampling rate is necessary to ensure that amplitude errors are small. It should be noted that amplitude errors will be introduced if the pressure and temperature sensors are not adequately chosen to measure this phenomenon. However, these frequencies are considered low enough that sensor response should not be a significant factor.

B.3.3 Control Implications

While it is not our intention to discuss control systems in detail, it is both appropriate and reasonable that we include a discussion in this section under analysis since the control requirements may significantly impact the system design. Here, we limit our discussion to air velocity control.

Air velocity is controlled by varying the speed of the tunnel's fan and, as we stated earlier, is computed using Bernoulli's equation in conjunction with measurements of dynamic pressure, total temperature, and static pressure. Since this is an existing facility, there is a closed-loop fan speed controller in existence, which is to remain intact. The new system will be integrated with the existing fan speed control system by automatically supplying analog speed set points as required to set and regulate velocity.

The set of requirements we impose on the system design, and necessary to implement continuous real-time air velocity control, are:

- Measure pressures and temperature

- Compute velocity

- Compare present velocity to desired velocity and establish error

- Determine fan speed required to correct this error and output new set point

- Repeat these steps continuously

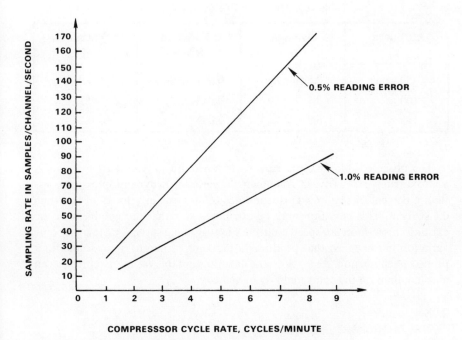

**Figur B.3. Required Channel Sampling Rate
to Achieve Specified Amplitude Accuracy**

While the steps appear simple, there are several areas that must be analyzed and these results incorporated into the system design. Specifically, our concerns relate to how well we can measure dynamic pressure and thus compute velocity and to the sensitivity of dynamic pressure to fan speed. As we will see, these affect the functional design.

1. Measurement Accuracy

We addressed measurement accuracy previously and determined that we can use a capacitance manometer with integral signal conditioning and conversion to provide a measurement uncertainty in dynamic pressure that is less than ± 0.1 percent of reading. This analysis, however, excludes any inaccuracy that may be caused by variations in the measurement phenomenon or electrical noise. We know in practice that measurement variations will exist, and thus we need to consider this when designing a system. Our concerns are with both amplitude and frequency.

In establishing requirements, the existing air speed turbulence was determined by observing the time variations in the dynamic pressure at three different constant fan speeds. These data are summarized in Table B.2.

Table B.2. Dynamic Pressure Variations

Air Speed, V	Dynamic q	q Variation, RMS	V Variation, %
50 kph	0.8 mmHg	0.007 mmHg	0.4
100	3.2	0.014	0.2
145	6.5	0.035	0.2

The observed dynamic pressure variation frequency for all air speeds is approximately 1.5–2.0 hertz. As shown, the variation in dynamic pressure is less than 1 percent of reading. This translates to an error in velocity of less than 0.4 percent. This variation may be attributed to either the goodness of the existing closed-loop fan speed controller in regulating speed (i.e., there is some variation in fan speed that produces a pressure variation) or to some other process phenomenon. Regardless, the magnitude of this variation represents an absolute limit on the controllability of velocity.

2. Bandwidth

The frequency of the observed variation in q of 1.5–2.0 hertz, coupled with a typical 2 Hz update rate of the sensor's digital output, presents a problem if the digital signal is to be used for q. With an assumed integration interval of 250 ms, attenuation of the observed low frequency variation (1.5–2.0 Hz), which results from the integration technique, is less than 30 dB. Consequently, the digital output will attempt to follow the disturbance. Since a stable value of q is essential for the controller, either smoothing of the measured q must be performed or the control tolerance must be set accordingly. As an alternative to using a sensor with a digital output, we can elect to use an analog signal and digitize this for control purposes. To prevent aliasing, the sampling frequency and filter must be chosen to provide the desired attenuation of the 1.5–2.0 hertz variation without introducing aliasing. However, using a filter with cutoff frequency sufficiently near zero so as to provide adequate attenuation may not be practical. In all likelihood, some form of digital smoothing must be implemented. Even so, precautions must be taken to ensure aliasing does not occur.

3. Resolution

Our concern here is in determining the minimum incremental voltage that, when input to the existing fan speed controller, will produce an incremental change in speed and thus velocity. In the computer mode, the set point to the closed-loop controller will be derived from a digital-to-analog converter. There is an inherent resolution associated with this device. We can use this in conjunction with the fan speed to q characteristics to define the control algorithm.

There is a resolution associated with the measurement of dynamic pressure that must be considered for control purposes. The precision of the measurement can be computed using the elemental random errors associated with both the sensor and data conditioning and then used to estimate effective measurement resolution. The value used should be at least ±3 sigma. No control action should be taken for errors in q that are less than this value.

4. Loop Update Time

To determine how often the sequence of control requirements listed in Section B.3.3 must be repeated, we need to be concerned with several issues. First, at what rate must we sample the inputs to ensure that our average will not be distorted at zero frequency and thus contain a bias? Second, how long does it take for the tunnel to reach a new velocity after a change in fan speed set point has been issued? Answering the second question requires that we know both the time constant of the tunnel and the time constant of the dynamic pressure measurements. This was experimentally determined by applying a step input to the existing fan speed controller and was found to be three seconds. Thus, the tunnel reached a new equilibrium in three seconds as established by monitoring the rate-of-change of dynamic pressure.

B.4 SUMMARY

A system configuration and its associated performance characteristics such as accuracy and speed can only be determined after the major issues have been analyzed. For this example, the analyses above, which are incomplete, may suggest that it is more feasible to implement the different controls with stand-alone controllers rather than with a central minicomputer system. However, this can not be established until the various analysis have been performed.

While we have only touched on the specifics for this application, the approach should be clear — establish requirements, perform analysis, establish a configuration, and choose equipment. Because engineers are a pragmatic lot, our first tendency is to draw block diagrams. Unfortunately, these oftentimes become the configuration with all subsequent design activities oriented towards making this work.